THE
FOOD ALLERGY COOKBOOK

A Guide to Living with Allergies and Entertaining with Healthy, Delicious Meals

CARMEL NELSON AND AMRA IBRISIMOVIC

Skyhorse Publishing

Skyhorse Publishing books may be purchased in bulk at special discounts for sales promotion, corporate gifts, fundraising, or educational purposes. Special editions can also be created to specifications. For details, contact the Special Sales Department, Skyhorse Publishing, 307 West 36th Street, 11th Floor, New York, NY 10018 or info@skyhorsepublishing.com.

Skyhorse® and Skyhorse Publishing® are registered trademarks of Skyhorse Publishing, Inc.®, a Delaware corporation.

www.skyhorsepublishing.com

10 9 8 7 6 5 4 3 2 1

Library of Congress Cataloging-in-Publication Data

Nelson, Carmel.

The food allergy cookbook : A Guide to Living with Allergies and Entertaining with Healthy, Delicious Meals / Carmel Nelson and Amra Ibrisimovic.

p. cm.

Includes index.

ISBN 978-1-61608-297-0 (hardcover : alk. paper)

1. Food allergy--Diet therapy--Recipes. I. Ibrisimovic, Amra. II. Title.

RC588.D53N45 2011

641.5'6318--dc22

2010053879

Printed in China

Photo credits:
Loria Chaddon: pp. 21, 22, 25, 26, 29, 49, 50, 53, 54, 57.
Amra Ibrisimovic: pp. 30, 35, 36, 39, 40,43, 44, 46, 53, 62, 64, 70, 77, 81, 86, 94, 97, 101, 102, 105, 106, 109, 131, 140, 147, 151, 152, 155, 159, 168, 172, 175, 176, 179, 183, 192, 195, 196, 200, 203, 207, 208, 215, 216, 224, 227, 228, 231.
Carmel Nelson: pp. 32, 61, 66, 69, 73, 82, 85, 89, 110, 116, 119, 120, 123, 124, 127, 128, 132, 135, 136, 144, 148, 160, 163, 164, 167, 171, 180, 184, 187, 188, 191, 199, 204, 211, 212, 219, 220, 222, 232
Donovan Worrell: pp. 78, 93, 98, 115, 139, 143.

Carmel dedicates this book to her parents—her mom, who taught her how to cook, and her father, who taught her how *not* to cook. Thanks, Mom and Dad; I love you!

Contents

Acknowledgments   iv

Chapter One: Our Stories   1

Chapter Two: Kitchen Tips   7

Chapter Three: Doctors and Medication   11

Chapter Four: Traveling with Food Allergies   14

Chapter Five: Holiday Menus   19

    Winter Holiday   19

    Thanksgiving   33

    Spring Holiday   47

Chapter Six: Soups   59

Chapter Seven: Appetizers   75

Chapter Eight: Salads and Side Dishes   91

Chapter Nine: Entrees   113

Chapter Ten: Pastries and Desserts   157

Helpful Websites and Books   234

Recipe Index   235

Acknowledgments

We would like to acknowledge the assistance of our friends and family who have aided us in our journey in discovering, cooking, and in producing this book. Thank you so much for your help, guidance, and photographic and artistic support, as well as your welcomed acceptance of all the goodies and leftovers! Thanks, also, for the artistic and photographic support of Donovan Worrell, Loria Chaddon, Don Wilson, and Tug Arkan. We couldn't have done this without you!

CHAPTER ONE

Our Stories

Foods and flavors are what help to distinguish cultures around the world. Celebrations involving food are universal, but not everyone can partake of the victuals due to the health risks certain foods pose. As children, we often learn our eating habits, food preferences, and food preparation skills by observing our parents. The following are Amra's and Carmel's stories of living with food allergies.

Amra's Story

All my life I was surrounded by great cooks. Each woman in my family was praised by the rest of her kinfolk for one dish or another. At family gatherings, each woman would bring one of her specialty dishes for the rest to enjoy. Unlike most children who only visit their grandparents on weekends or holidays, I lived with my grandparents. In Bosnian culture, families are close knit and hold high regard for all elders. Generations gather regularly for lunch, afternoon coffee, or just to visit. Thus, in my household, we had visitors every single day. Everyone was greeted with open arms and delicious smells coming from my grandmother's kitchen. Having warm and delectable meals available at a moment's notice eliminated the necessity for one to learn how to cook. Looking back on it, I probably never would have learned if I had not had an allergic reaction to the food I was served.

In April of 2000, after dining out with my high school friend Carmel, I had a severe allergic reaction and immediately went to the doctor's office. As part of a follow-up treatment, I was given an allergy skin test. Though I tested positive to some environmental allergens, as well as wheat, the cause of the anaphylaxis was never determined. I was given an Epi-pen and trained in how to use it in case of another severe reaction. I was also put on antihistamines to help with the environmental allergens. However, I never received any information on food allergies, nutrition, or dietary restriction.

In the months that followed I turned from a happy college graduate with a fabulous new job to a miserable hypochondriac; my body was constantly covered in hives due to ongoing allergic reactions to unknown causes. My sinuses were constantly inflamed and I started feeling lethargic, achy, and found myself falling asleep behind my computer after my lunch hour. Every time my colleagues and I would go out for Italian food at lunch, I would later have horrible cramps and spend most of the afternoon traveling between my office and the ladies' room. My doctor could never find anything wrong with me, though, no matter how frequently I visited his office.

Around this time I also started to gain weight. Once I reached an all-time high of 160 pounds, I decided to start looking for a diet that was affordable and easy to maintain. In my quest for a diet formula that would help me go from size 14 back to size 9, I became an avid magazine reader. Eventually I found *Woman's World* magazine. I tried diet after diet, learning more about food and health along the way. Then one week I ran across an article on allergies and food intolerance, which gave helpful information on food elimination diets and I decided to try it out. After a few weeks on the elimination diet, a completely new world opened in front of my eyes. This new world was both scary and beautiful. I began losing weight and also discovered that my gastro-intestinal difficulties were not imaginary. I learned that I am not a hypochondriac but rather a person with multiple food allergies and intolerances. As I continued to eliminate certain foods from my daily diet, I became more energetic, my skin cleared up, and my hives were more manageable. Once again I was able to concentrate, complete my work in a timely manner, and my mood also improved. By following the elimination diet I learned that I could not eat wheat, barley, dairy, soy, or corn. Armed with this new knowledge I decided to take charge of my life in regards to food and eating.

The first step was to become more educated on allergies. To my surprise there was an amazing scarcity of information on food allergies available to the general public. Judging by my experiences with medical professionals, most of them seemed to be in the dark on this topic as well. Nevertheless, I was fortunate enough to run into the book titled *The False Fat Diet*, by Elson M. Haas, MD, and Cameron Stauth. This book became my go-to cookbook, my personal doctor, and my best companion. With this book in hand I set out on a search for an allergist with knowledge and experience in treating food allergies.

The second and most difficult step was to make my newfound diet a lifestyle. Eating fresh or boiled fruits and vegetables with a piece of meat seasoned with salt and pepper cooked on a George Foreman grill was all right for a while. The food costs were affordable, and meals were done in minutes. Extra pounds were melting like a snowman on a sunny day. However, after some time, the food I was eating became rather boring.

While my family of great cooks was preparing and consuming scrumptious foods and pastries that I had grown to love as a child, I found I had to nibble on hard, store-bought rice bread and concentrate with all my might on not giving in to temptation and join them. Family gatherings became torture sessions. I was always

nudged by someone to try at least a bite of something that they had made. Coming from a culture where food is an expression of love, caring, respect, and family, it is very painful not to be able to participate in this exchange.

Even more challenging was eating in social gatherings outside the family circle. Food habits are particularly noticeable during business lunches, dates, and social gatherings. People often asked if I was on a starvation diet and I found it awkward to explain why I couldn't eat certain foods. I worried about creating poor first impressions with a prospective manager, employer, or even a date due to my peculiar food choices.

Even more difficult was the routine of buying snacks, pre-made meals, and junk food. I found it very hard to find a product that was free of all my food allergens. The lack of allergy-free products available at stores, which when

found are often only semi-edible, made me seek out cookbooks in order to prepare my own dishes.

I found that each new book, each new article, and each new recipe that did not quite work for my taste buds taught me to persevere, and built a desire to keep trying new recipes. In my attempts to be able to eat food that looks, smells, and tastes good, I started to learn how to cook. This wasn't easy, as there were more failures than successes in the kitchen. If I had saved every loaf of bread that turned out like a brick I could have built a spare bedroom by now. However, with time I started to get the hang of it. I am fortunate to be surrounded by friends willing to help with advice, research, and testing my food projects. Some friends were great supports, asking when I would try a new recipe, and eager to taste the finished product. Other friends, like Carmel, suggested that these new recipes should be compiled into a book and shared with others like us.

Carmel's Story

Like Amra, food and the culture surrounding it has always been integral to my upbringing. Although my discovery of food allergies does not have the drama of Amra's anaphylaxis, I too discovered my allergies later in life. This meant I had to re-learn the entire process of cooking and eating in order to accommodate my new diet. I learned about cooking from my mother—how to cook nutritious, tasty, and gourmet meals—and from my father, how *not* to cook, as he tended to create inedible combinations of foods and flavors, served bizarre portions, and frequently engaged in culinary abuses.

I grew up in a traditional suburban American home with both parents working, and my sister and I were "latchkey kids." When I was younger, I'd sit in the kitchen, watching my mom cook meals, learning the tricks of the trade, then putting those new skills to practice with batches of chocolate chip cookies, bowls of soup, and lots of grilled cheese sandwiches. As I grew older, my parents took to working later at night, which meant that my sister and I had to help out with the chores. We alternated the chore of loading dirty dishes, a task I did not particularly enjoy, with sticky plates crusted with icky food particles. One day I proposed to my parents a switch in the assigned jobs; I would take over cooking the family meals in lieu of washing dishes. I was ten years old at the time. Having observed my mother for many years, I knew the basics of cooking and I was proficient at reading and following recipes. By the age of twelve, I was cooking soufflés, roast chicken, and helping with the holiday meals.

My father, on the other hand, taught me the very helpful skill of how *not* to cook, with an incident that has become a family legend of sorts. I was two years old, but my older sister remembers the day very well. A warning to readers: Do not try this recipe at home!

My mother was finishing graduate school and Dad was working as Mr. Mom. He had recently purchased a crock pot—a newfangled kitchen toy—and wanted to experiment with it. Setting the crock pot on low that morning, he added frozen pork chops, a large can of peaches (with the juice), and a can of tomato paste. That evening, as we approached our home, a foul stench permeated through the brick of the house exterior, creating fumes that might concern a Hazmat team. My sister and I were then forced to sit at the table and eat this toxic concoction, whose texture was that of lumpy and acidic wallpaper paste. My father had several servings in an attempt to show his dear daughters how tasty this treat was. Some thirty years later, my sister still will not eat meat with fruit. I will not let my father cook; and he has finally admitted, "It seemed like a good idea at the time, but I guess it was pretty bad." Dad has continued to make other awful brews, some too frightening and distasteful to mention.

Then, several years ago, I returned from a much needed vacation to Hawaii. While on vacation in the tropics, I mainly ate fruit and fresh fish, as these foods are scarcer in winter in Alaska, where I currently reside. I had not had any exposure to dairy while I was away, a fact I later discovered. Returning home, I resumed my normal eating habits, only to find myself in the emergency room—twice—with horrible cramping and terrible abdominal pain. Apparently the fruit and fish diet of Hawaii had cleaned my system of dairy, and the return to my accustomed food preferences created the ideal environment for the development of a severe reaction to dairy. I went to several doctors, who told me

I was lactose intolerant. I tried Lactaid, only to find myself back in the emergency room.

Eventually I found a naturopathic physician, who taught me some things about the gastrointestinal system. I also had been in close contact with Amra and spoke with her about her experiences with food allergies. She directed me to some great books, including *The False Fat Diet*, where I learned about elimination diets and more technical knowledge of allergies. I tried the elimination diet and learned I was not only allergic to dairy but also to wheat, oats, and barley. I was devastated. All of the comfort foods I had grown up eating were suddenly off limits: no more grilled cheese sandwiches, clam chowder, chocolate chip cookies, ice cream, or cheese cake. Finding foods safe to eat was a real challenge in the beginning. There were times in those early months of food allergies that I thought all I could

eat was rabbit food and steamed rice… blah!

Amra and I commiserated on the serious lack of prepared foods available and also on the lack of cookbooks on food allergies. We found some cookbooks that focused on wheat- and gluten-free, some on dairy- and nut-free, but few were comprehensive enough for multiple food allergy sufferers. I found myself challenged like I had never been before. I thought I knew a lot about cooking, but as I experimented in the kitchen, I realized how complex food chemistry truly is. Amra and I began comparing notes on recipes—what worked and what didn't. Some days I ended up with slop, other days boot leather. Rarely was anything appetizing. But eventually I began to learn the art of allergy-free cooking.

Amra and I also shared the isolation we felt due to our inability to participate in food gatherings.

We discussed the etiquette of refusing food in social situations due to our food allergies and how hard it was to risk our health versus the benefits of social dining. At work, lunches with colleagues became difficult; potluck dinners, social evenings out with friends, and family meals were real struggles. How does one say, "No thank you. I can't eat that. It will make me sick"? Particularly painful was eating with our families, who raised us on traditional foods and didn't understand why we suddenly refused to eat our favorite meals. They felt their love offerings were rejected; we were torn. The pressures created from these social situations became as big as, if not bigger than, the problem of the food allergies themselves. Amra and I knew how to avoid certain foods when we cooked, but when the food was prepared for us, it became a health- and life-threatening issue.

Our Stories, Shared

We were inspired by our personal struggles and decided to write a book that would be helpful for individuals who suffer from food allergies, while at the same time finally addressing the social factor in which food allergies play, an issue not discussed in any other literature on the subject.

You will find in these pages numerous recipes, often of the dessert variety (as these foods are particularly dangerous for food allergy sufferers), as well as menus for major American holiday meals. Scattered throughout the book are helpful ideas for handling eating in social situations. These tips will provide you with information on graciously handling well-meaning friends and family who offer potentially dangerous foods to the allergy sufferer, as well as ideas for traveling, ordering at restaurants, and negotiating the tantalizing selections offered at potluck dinners. In compiling this book we hope to help others learn how to maneuver successfully through the challenges of food allergies, and to eat well in the process.

CHAPTER TWO

Kitchen Tips

One thing we have learned in writing this book is how few resources there are out there on food allergies. It's not uncommon for people to be allergic to one food, but the issue of multiple food allergies poses a serious problem for people who like to eat—as we do. When you find yourself faced with allergies to cooking staples, such as wheat, dairy, soy, corn, barley, and oats, meal options become very limited. And as the American diet has become even more commercialized, it is even harder to avoid potential food allergens. Many foods are pre-packaged, loaded with preservatives and fillers, and often those additives are the causes of most food allergies. Corn syrup is everywhere, from the glue on the back of stamps, to candy, to sodas, to most desserts. Wheat is also hard to avoid, as it is the basis for almost all baked goods. Dairy leaks its way into foods in insidious ways from fillers in processed meats (casein) to dough conditioners. Soy is a common additive as it is a form of instant protein, is low fat, and is inexpensive.

Trying to avoid these staples becomes a full time job, particularly challenging in our fast-paced society. We like foods premade because we appreciate the convenience. We recognize that cooking from scratch is one of the hardest parts of having a food allergy. We hope that the following tips will ease some of the burden, and save some time in the kitchen.

Food Labels

In 2006, the Food Allergen Labeling and Consumer Protection Act (FALCPA) was passed, which requires all purchased foods to list the most common allergens (the top eight are milk, eggs, fish, crustacean shellfish, tree nuts, peanuts [a legume], wheat, and soybeans [another legume]). However, there is no requirement as to how companies list these allergens. You may find some labels that state "made in a facility that processes milk products and nuts." Cross contamination is also a constant threat. If you're unsure about a packaged product, try to contact the food maker directly, or simply avoid that product. Fortunately, there *is* more attention being paid to food allergies in packaged food, and the FDA is considering strengthening requirements for labels. For the latest information on federal labeling guidelines, go to http://www.cfsan.fda.gov.

Milk

Milk products are often used as fillers in other foods. Obviously, if you are allergic to milk or dairy, avoid all milk (including buttermilk, acidophilus milk, dried milk powder and protein, and evaporated and condensed milk), malts, milkshakes, ice cream, yogurt, cheese, cream sauces, sour cream, creamers, half and half, puddings, most desserts,

and butter. Also watch labels for various milk derivatives. They often hide in things like margarine, protein bars and drinks, processed meats, "dairy-free" cheeses (which contain casein), and "non dairy" creamers. Some cereals also contain dairy fillers. Here are the names to look for on labels:

- Casein and Sodium Caseinates
- Lactoglobulin
- Lactolbumin
- Lactose
- Milk Powder
- Whey (including powder and solids)

Soy

Unlike milk, soy is often easy to find on food labels. Avoid foods that are obviously soy, such as tofu, soy sauce (or any Asian foods due to the high likelihood of soy in the ingredients), soy yogurt, soy milk and cheeses, whipped toppings, drinks, and soybeans.

Also watch out for tempeh, miso, and soy lecithin. Soy products are often used as protein fillers, so be wary of protein drinks or shakes and protein bars. Sometimes processed foods add TVP (textured vegetable protein), which is typically soy based.

Corn

Corn is everywhere. Corn syrup is typically used as an alternative sweetener in foods because it is very cheap and readily available. Because of this, candy should be avoided, as corn syrup is likely to be first on the ingredients list. Boxed cake mixes, puddings, and desserts in general will likely contain corn syrup. Also watch out for ketchup, barbeque sauces, and cereals. Avoid obvious corn foods including tortillas, corn chips, corn bread, popcorn, and corn starch. Corn starch sometimes hides in products in the baking aisle. It is contained in baking powder and gravy mixes and used as a means of keeping dry ingredients dry (marshmallows, powdered sugar, and occasionally pre-mixed seasonings). You can purchase baking powder without corn starch, or make your own by mixing two parts cream of tartar, one part baking soda, and two parts arrowroot powder (*The Complete Food Allergy Cookbook*, Marilyn Gioannini). Corn oils should also be avoided, including some vegetable oils and shortenings. Also look for the following names by which corn may appear on food labels:

- Dextrin
- Dextrose
- Fructose
- Maize
- Maltodextrins
- Mannitol
- Sorbitol

Wheat or Gluten

If you are allergic to wheat or gluten, you might also want to avoid oats, barley, and rye. Often these grains are processed in the same factories and you run a high risk of cross contamination. You should generally stay away from baked goods, breads, and pastas as these all contain wheat or gluten. However, wheat also likes to hide under other names:

- Dextrin
- Hydrolyzed plant protein (HPP)
- Hydrolyzed vegetable protein (HVP)
- Malt
- Maltodextrin
- Modified food starch
- "Natural flavoring"

Other Allergens

If you are allergic to shellfish or seafood, avoid anything with gills. If you're allergic to iodine (typically found in seawater), be sure to purchase only non-iodized salt. Nuts tend to be found in cookies, cakes, and pastries, but nut oils are often used in cooking. Peanut oil is very common in Asian cuisine. You might find it easier to stick to safflower or olive oil. Be wary of certain medicines and supplements as they might contain fillers, which are laden with allergens. The topic of medications will be addressed in Chapter 3.

Stocking Your Pantry

We have discovered some very necessary foods to keep stocked in your pantry. Most of these products are readily available in larger grocery stores and health food stores. The following list should get you on your way to cooking up some tasty treats.

- Agar
- Arrowroot Flour
- Butter flavoring (similar to an extract)
- Coconut milk
- Cottonseed shortening
- Dried egg replacement
- Flax seed
- Garfava flour

- Brown and white sugars
- Gelatin
- Glutinous rice flour
- Guar gum
- Milk substitute (such as rice milk)
- Olive and canola oils
- Potato flour
- Potato starch
- Pure vanilla extract
- Quinoa
- Rice flour
- Safflower margarine
- Sorghum flour
- Sweet rice flour
- Tapioca flour/starch
- Vinegar
- Xanthan gum

A few other tips for stocking your kitchen include keeping a regular supply of gallon-size freezer zip-lock bags and a permanent marker. These are used to label the different types of white powder stocking your cabinets. You wouldn't want to confuse the flours as they serve different purposes. The advantage of the zip-lock bags is that they take up less storage space in your kitchen. Plastic storage containers can also be used if you prefer. Speaking from experience, be sure to securely close all bags of flour before shaking them or storing them, otherwise you might end up in a snow storm! Periodically, you will need to switch out the bags for newer ones.

Flour Mixture

This recipe is a basis for most of the baked goods in this cookbook. It is a slightly altered version of Bette Hagman's (*The Gluten Free Gourmet*). It will be referred to in recipes as the "Flour Mixture."

INGREDIENTS:

- 3 cups rice flour
- 3 cups tapioca flour
- 3 cups potato starch
- 3 tablespoons potato flour

Mix these flours together and label the bag as a basic flour mixture. This mixture usually works as a direct replacement for wheat flour.

A Note on Our Recipes

As you can see by the recipes, we have tried diligently to remove the major food allergens from each dish. For some recipes, you have the option of adding certain foods such as corn, shellfish, nuts, and nut flavorings if you desire. If you are allergic to these foods, simply leave out those optional ingredients. Some of our recipes do have nuts or peanuts as a main ingredient. If you are allergic, avoid these recipes. If you are also allergic to eggs, there are egg substitutions available in supermarkets that may work for you. Sometimes an egg replacement mixture can be created from flax seed. For the substitution of one egg, take one tablespoon of flax seed and one cup boiling water. Let it sit for five minutes. However, if you are allergic to eggs, recipes like Crème Brûlée and Yorkshire Pudding may have to be avoided altogether, as eggs are a key ingredient.

CHAPTER THREE

Doctors and Medication

*Please note: Amra and I are **not** physicians, pharmacists, allergists, or experts on allergies beyond what we have learned from our own personal experiences and through hours of reading. We strongly recommend working closely with your physicians and pharmacist to address all medical concerns.*

As we have already laid out in the previous chapters, food allergies and intolerances are and will always be a major imposition on your daily life. As a social worker, I (Carmel) am very familiar with navigating through the labyrinths of the medical, social service, and governmental worlds. I have become skilled at advocacy, translating "medical speak" into "normal speak," and knowing what questions to ask and how to ask them of the various providers I see. I will try to pass along some of that practical knowledge to you. First, and foremost, become familiar with your body, your habits, your symptoms, your food choices, any medications you may be taking, and your medical history. Spend the time to gather your own health records, and develop a "Quick Guide" for your history. Note dates of surgeries, diagnoses, major tests, hospital stays, and all medications (yes, even over-the-counter medications) you may be taking (including dosage and frequency of use). Have this Quick Guide saved on a computer, ready to update and print off for any new physician you see. It's also wise to keep a current copy of this record with you at all times.

One suggested format is:

Name: John Smith
Address: 123 Maple Lane, Any City, State, Zip
Phone: (555) 555-5555
Emergency Contact: Sally Smith, Mother, (555) 555-1111
Insurance Information: Insurance Company A, # 1234-5678

List all medications, dosage, frequency of use
Asprin 25 mg 1 pill every morning
Antibiotic 200 mg 1 pill four times daily

PRNs: Ibuprofen, Acetaminophen

Name/Phone of all Doctors
Dr. Jones (Primary Physician) (555) 555-2222
Dr. Williams (Allergist) (555) 555-3333
Dr. Bates (Orthopedics) (555) 555-4444

Pharmacy: All Drugs Rx (555) 555-6666

Medical History
4/02 Apendectomy, St. Luke's Hospital, Any City USA
5/03 Diagnosed with Allergies to Wheat, Milk, and Nuts
6/04 Broken Left Wrist

This Quick Guide will become part of your medical record, making tracking your medical history, medications, and concerns easier for you and your physicians.

Second, when working with your doctors, be sure to sign releases of information so that different doctors can and do share medical information about you. Encourage the doctors to speak with each other and coordinate care. This prevents potential hazards such as over-prescribing medication, encountering conflicts of medical treatment, and ensuring you receive top quality care.

Third, when you are at a doctor appointment, bring a list of questions or concerns and have notepaper ready to write down answers. Also, ask for definitions and explanations to any terms you do not know. When you get home, research what you have learned. Doctors only do half the healing; you do the other half. There are some great websites for learning about medical diagnoses, medications, and procedures (reference them in the appendix of this book).

Fourth, become familiar with your pharmacist. Get to know him or her by name. Have all your prescriptions filled at the same pharmacy. This ensures that you receive the attention you need and prevents mix-ups from occurring. As part of knowing your medications, take the time to ask questions of the pharmacy staff, read the prescription inserts, and learn about the side effects of the medications you are taking.

Most importantly, take note of the inactive ingredients in all your medications. I have learned by experience that there are thousands of pharmaceutical companies and hundreds of generic formulas for one drug. The main ingredient may be the same, but the fillers used to create the pills can be very different. Fillers often contain the following ingredients, but are not limited to: milk (anahydrose lactate, lactose monohydrate, lactose), corn (corn starch, corn syrup, dextrose), soy (soy lecithin), and so on. These fillers can and likely will be present in over-the-counter medications as well. Read the labels and ask for help if you need it. Be sure to explain to your pharmacist your allergies to these products. Often you will be asked, "Are you allergic to any medications?" but this doesn't imply the ingredients in those medications. Also, one really helpful resource is www.drugs.com, which is the most up-to-date list of medications, prescription and over-the-counter. You can look up everything related to medications including inactive ingredients. Be proactive and do the research for yourself rather that depending entirely on your doctors or pharmacist.

Finally, be prepared that some medical professionals do not like curious patients. You might find some "old school" doctors who do not like to talk to patients, offer detailed explanations, and who expect that they should just be able to "do" to you. Do *not* tolerate that! *You* are the expert on *your* body, and good doctors understand that without patient compliance and understanding, whatever they prescribe for treatment will only work if you are part of the equation. Advocate for yourself and your rights; learn about your medical condition; ask questions; be an active participant in your own treatment.

With these basic premises, you will likely find that maneuvering through the maze of medical care will be much easier. Often, as people develop medical problems, they compound one on top of another. This isn't necessarily the body's failing, but rather the start of a line of knowledge. As you become skilled in negotiating your medical care, your quality of care and life will improve and you will feel in control of your body and your life—a crucial life lesson for everyone.

CHAPTER FOUR

Traveling with Food Allergies

Since September 11, 2001, traveling anywhere in the world has become significantly more complex for all of us. Traveling with food allergies adds to the complexity. Whether traveling by air, car, or train, preparing and planning will make for much more pleasant travels and safer trips.

Ideally, planning for vacations starts at a minimum of three months prior to your departure date, but sometimes leaving for a trip is more sudden. If you do not travel often, it can be particularly stressful if you're not familiar with packing, negotiating airports, and sleeping in another bed. If you are a frequent traveler you likely have packing down to a science, knowing how to fit everything into the suitcase to maximize space. Amra and I have always found it helpful to bring extra zip-top bags (they come in handy for all sorts of things), Benadryl, juice-box-size rice milk, a set of plastic silverware, and a small "pharmacy" of over-the-counter medications for the emergency "what-ifs" and "whens" that tend to occur when out of town. If you have difficulty figuring out what these things might be for you, consider what you tend to use on a monthly basis in your medicine cabinet and pack those items. It's much more comfortable to have these items on hand than to have to hunt them down when you are not feeling well in an unfamiliar location.

When planning trips, consider where you will be lodging. It is advisable to look for lodging that offers kitchens, such as vacation condos or hotels with kitchenettes. These types of lodgings allow for you to prepare meals as you would at home, reducing the potential for allergy exposure. You can also look for places that have groceries nearby. Hotel chains that offer kitchens include Extended Stay, Homestead, Hyatt, and Candlewood Suites. If looking for vacation condominiums, Craigslist can be a helpful resource but it's worth sticking with reputable companies that have been established with the Better Business Bureau or AAA, rather than sending money to a complete stranger and being taken to the cleaners.

Addressing meals with food allergies while traveling is always a struggle. If traveling by car, rail, or plane, the likelihood is, more often than not, you will encounter fast food and chain restaurants. Consider packing snacks for yourself such as dried fruit or fruit that can travel well—apples, pears, or oranges (bananas bruise too easily). If flying, remember the TSA guidelines about what will pass through security screenings (i.e., no liquids). Try to pre-plan your trip with stops for meals in mind. You can also usually check online for information on which restaurants are available at your airport (or connecting airports), previewing opportunities for meals, and packing accordingly. Consider using

iPhone or web applications, such as urbanspoon.com or opentable.com, to look at restaurants' menus and for restaurants that may be gluten free. Some chain restaurants have already begun offering alternative menus for individuals with special diets, such as Boston Market, Chili's Grill and Bar, Olive Garden, P. F. Chang's China Bistro, Uno Chicago Grill, Wendy's (yes, the fast food joint!), and Z Pizza.

If you are traveling to a foreign destination and you are not fluent in that country's language, it is crucial to be prepared for the foods and allergies. A helpful thing to do prior to your trip is to have business cards made (on florescent cardstock if possible) that list your allergies in that country's language. You can use foreign translation applications found online to translate your allergies into any language. Learn some key phrases regarding your allergies while you're at it (e.g., "sans gluten?"). Use your

computer to create the business cards then have them printed at Kinkos. When at a restaurant, hand those cards to the wait-staff or chef to aid you in preventing allergy exposures. Models for these cards can be found at www. foodallergy.org/files/media/ chefcard1/chefcardtemplate.pdf. When eating at restaurants, be sure to inform the wait staff, and if possible the chef, of your allergies via the cards, asking which items on the menus are recommended for you. This brings their attention to your allergies directly. You might even find a unique dish not mentioned on the menu that you can enjoy eating!

If flying, it's advisable to check with your airline regarding whether or not they have continued the practice of serving nuts during the flight. Advise the airline of your allergies when making reservations, when you check in for your flight, and also when you board to reduce the risk of peanuts or other nuts being served on the flight. This may seem to be "overkill" but it's worth being overly safe than sorry. Be sure to pack and have your Epi-pen available at all times. TSA also needs to be informed that you are carrying an Epi-pen when you go through the security checkpoint. Be sure to pack all your medications in your carryon luggage as well, as sometimes baggage does not make the destination at the same time you do. Using medisets is a smart way to pack medications as it reduces the space used in your luggage (the other advantage to this is that you have access to your scheduled medications while flying, particularly if on a long flight). Label the medisets with all names of medications and doses, and also have a master list of medications, doses, and prescribing doctors in case you do have to access medical care while away from home. If you take liquid medications, these

need to be packaged separately in your carryon luggage. Use of zip-top bags for these is always smart as it helps the TSA with their screening process. It's recommended to keep all medications together in a section of your bag with easy access, as these will need to be removed for screening. Many airports have "sniffers" for liquid medications. Any injectable medications also need to be inspected.

Wherever you opt to go, do not let food allergies limit your travels. There are numerous destinations that are allergy friendly and welcoming; some cater to families with special needs, including allergies. Consider cruises or Disney vacations, as both are very adept at accommodating food allergies. Disney has two theme parks, one resort in Hawaii, and a cruise line in the United States. If looking at the theme parks as a family vacation you can stay at

one of the Disney resort lodges, purchasing packages that include entrance into the parks and dining plans. Disney's dining plans do offer options for special diets including for those with food allergies (http://disneyworld. disney.go.com/wdw/common/ guestServicesDetail?id=Guest ServicesSpecialDietaryDetailP age&bhcp=1). All it takes is to contact Guest Services and the Disney Reservation Center prior to arrival and inform them of the allergies, making reservations for sit-down meals. Once you arrive at the restaurants your allergies will have already been noted on your hotel card and the Disney "Cast Members" (aka wait staff) will already have the information. Frequently the restaurant chef will come to the table to confirm the dietary restrictions and meals will be prepared to order. The meal plans also offer snacks throughout the day and there are places in the parks where you can obtain allergy-free snacks made by Divvies, Enjoy Life, Kinnikinnik, Namaste, and EnerG foods. If ever a family vacation can be created for a family with special dietary needs, Disney has done it. Parents have even created their own website to talk about their reflections on the Disney experiences: http://allears.net. There is a wide range of resorts from value priced all the way up to luxury resorts. For someone looking for a fun vacation, free of the "headache" of food allergies, Disney is a safe bet.

If looking at taking a cruise, whichever cruise line you take, whichever destination you want to explore, the biggest thing to remember is to plan ahead. Cruising is a fun way to see parts of the world without having to pack and repack at each port of call. The food is typically fantastic and the accommodation is five-star. Cruise lines make their

money not on the cost of the trip but on the excursions and extras that you purchase. Booking a cruise through discount websites, such as Priceline or Orbitz, can be a great way to save money, sometimes allowing you to get a seven-day cruise for as little as $400 per person. Shop around online; sometimes work with a travel agent. Often your best prices will be found within six weeks of sailing. Once you have booked your cruise, be sure to write to the cruise customer service department, sometimes called the Food and Beverage Manager (once onboard), and advise them of your allergies, asking them for the name and email of the Maître d' of the ship so you can begin correspondence and prepare the head chef for your special diet. Once you have embarked, be sure to sign up for traditional dining ("standard restaurant experience"). Meet with the Maître d' as soon as possible once on board to remind

him or her of your allergies and s/he will advise the head chef and your identified waiter for your table at your assigned time for dinner. The advantage to this is that your waiter will become very familiar with you and your habits, learn your allergies, and be able to advise the chef. Often, they will become so familiar they will have your drinks waiting for you when you arrive for dinner! Meals on cruises are frequently designed for the day and patrons have choices for the meals from a short menu. With a special diet, you may get an opportunity to pre-select your meal a day ahead of time in case the chef needs to pick up ingredients at the next port of call. If you choose to approach the buffets on a cruise, be very careful as there is a high likelihood of cross-contamination and little opportunity to be aware of the hidden ingredients (unless you're just splurging on fresh fruit and veggies). It is also highly recommended to check in with the medical crew early on in the cruise in case of accidental allergy exposure. Advise them of your allergies, your cabin number, and your medications. If you choose to go on an excursion and have the option, take a box lunch from the ship rather than risking food at the port of call. The ship already has a record of your allergies so this reduces the risk of accidental exposure.

Although food allergies can and do create some challenges for travel, they should not prevent you from exploring new locales and taking trips abroad. With basic preparedness and planning you can safely have vacations and trips.

CHAPTER FIVE:

Holiday Menus

Winter Holiday

20	Prime Rib
23	Roasted Potatoes
24	Creamy Spinach
27	Yorkshire Pudding
28	Sweet Potato Pie
31	Aunt Nina's Apple Pastry
32	Leftover Prime Rib Stew

The Food Allergy Cookbook

Prime Rib

1 4–6 LBS RIB ROAST
1 BULB OF GARLIC, CRUSHED
1 LARGE YELLOW ONION, COARSELY CHOPPED
  SALT AND PEPPER
  OLIVE OIL
1 CUP BEEF BROTH
¼ CUP COLD WATER
1 TEASPOON POTATO OR TAPIOCA STARCH

1. Preheat oven to 325°F.

2. Begin by stabbing the rib roast repeatedly every few inches. Break apart the bulb of garlic into individual cloves and strip cloves of skins. Chop onion very coarsely, with sections of onion about ½ inch by 1 inch or so. Alternate placing onion and garlic cloves into stab holes of the roast.

3. Rub olive oil over entire roast and rub in salt and pepper onto roast. Place in a roast pan, elevated on a rack. Insert meat thermometer. Bake until roast cooks to 140°F for medium rare (about 2 to 2 ½ hours), 155°F for medium (2 ¼ hours to 3 ¼ hours).

4. Remove roast from oven, transfer to serving platter, and cover with foil for about 15 minutes, letting juices redistribute.

5. While roast rests, take the pan and deglaze with beef broth, making sure to scrape the pan for the crusty drippings. Quickly mix water and starch, creating a slurry. Add to the pan drippings. Cook to boiling and remove from heat. Use the pan gravy to top the thickly sliced rib roast.

6. Serve with Yorkshire Pudding and Roasted Potatoes.

Serves 6–10

Roasted Potatoes

1 LB WHITE POTATOES, PEELED
1 TABLESPOON FRESH ROSEMARY,
  CRUSHED
  SALT AND PEPPER TO TASTE
  OLIVE OIL

1. Preheat oven to 325°F.

2. Cut potatoes into quarters. Sprinkle potatoes with oil, salt, pepper, and rosemary.

3. Bake in oven along with rib roast if possible. Bake for 45 minutes.

Serves 6–10

Hot Tip:

Fresh herbs can be very expensive and are typically seasonal. To extend the life of fresh herbs, try freezing them in ice cube trays. For each cube, place one tablespoon of herbs and cover with water. Freeze then store separated cubes in zip top storage bags.

Creamy Spinach

10 OZ FROZEN SPINACH, CHOPPED
(DO NOT SUBSTITUTE WITH WHOLE
LEAVES)
3 MEDIUM CLOVES OF GARLIC,
CHOPPED
1 TABLESPOON OLIVE OIL
3 TABLESPOONS SWEET RICE FLOUR
½ CUP DILUTED COCONUT MILK (1
PART COCONUT MILK, 2 PARTS
WATER)
1 EGG, BEATEN
SALT TO TASTE

1. Defrost and drain spinach.

2. In a frying pan, over medium heat, brown garlic in oil. Stir in spinach and a pinch of salt. Cover the pan and let the spinach cook for a couple of minutes.

3. Mix rice flour and coconut milk, stirring until there are no lumps. Pour coconut milk and flour mixture into spinach and stir until all the liquid is absorbed.

4. Add beaten egg and stir until egg is cooked.

5. Can be served warm as a side dish, or cold as a dip.

Serves 4 (side dish) or 12 (dip)

Yorkshire Pudding

1 ⅓   CUPS FLOUR MIXTURE (SEE P.10)
½   TEASPOON SALT
3   EGGS, BEATEN
1 ½   CUPS MILK SUBSTITUTE
⅓   CUP MARGARINE

1. Preheat over to 400°F.

2. Split margarine between two 9-inch cake pans (you can also use large muffin tins or pop over pans for a different look). Place pans in oven as it preheats.

3. Mix flour and salt. Add beaten eggs and gradually whisk in milk. Pour batter into hot pans. Bake 40 to 45 minutes, or until golden brown.

4. Cut into wedges with shears or pizza cutter (if using muffin tins or pop overs skip this step).

5. Serve with rib roast au jus.

Serves 6

Sweet Potato Pie

2   PIE CRUSTS (SEE P.206)
2   16-OZ CANS OF COOKED SWEET
       POTATOES
⅔   CUP BROWN SUGAR
1 ½   TEASPOONS GROUND CINNAMON
1   TEASPOON FRESH GROUND
       GINGER
¼   TEASPOON CLOVE
¼   TEASPOON NUTMEG
3   EGGS, BEATEN
1   16-OZ CAN COCONUT MILK

1. Preheat oven to 350°F. Prepare and pre-bake pie crusts.

2. Blend all other ingredients together. Fill pie crusts and bake for 45 minutes to an hour, or until a knife comes out clean when inserted into the center.

Serves 12–16

Aunt Nina's Apple Pastry

Dough

2   CUPS FLOUR MIXTURE (SEE P. 10)
½   CUP POTATO STARCH
½   CUP TAPIOCA STARCH
1   CUP SUGAR
    8 OZ (2 STICKS) MARGARINE
1   EGG
1   EGG YOLK
1   TABLESPOON BAKING POWDER
    GRATED ZEST OF 1 LEMON
3   TABLESPOONS COCONUT MILK

Filling

6   MEDIUM APPLES, PEELED
    AND GRATED
    JUICE OF 1 LEMON
1 ½   CUPS SUGAR
½   STICK MARGARINE
    CINNAMON TO TASTE

1. Preheat the oven to 300°F.

2. Cook filling ingredients to soften but do not overcook.

3. In a bowl combine dry ingredients and set aside. In another bowl cream margarine, sugar, eggs, milk, and lemon zest. Using a mixer combine wet and dry ingredients. Split the dough in half. Using your fingers or a spatula, spread one half of the dough on the bottom of a greased 9 x 9 pan, then prick the dough with a fork. Cover it with filling. Roll out the remaining dough to the size of the pan.

4. Using a rolling mat carefully transfer the dough to the pan. Using a fork or toothpick prick the dough, so that the steam can escape. Bake it for 20 minutes or until golden brown.

5. Serve it warm with "Rice Dream" ice cream or serve cold. Either way, the pastry is soft and moist for more than a week.

Serves 6–10

Leftover Prime Rib Stew

BONES AND TOUGHER CUTS FROM
LEFTOVER PRIME RIB DINNER

½ LB POTATOES, PEELED AND CUT
INTO QUARTERS

5 CARROT STALKS, CUT INTO 2-INCH
SEGMENTS

1 CUP BEEF BROTH
SALT AND PEPPER TO TASTE

1. Combine all ingredients, cutting beef pieces into bite sized segments.

2. Place everything in a crock pot and set on low. Let the stew slow cook for about 4–5 hours. Gravy will thicken on its own.

3. Remove the bones from the stew. Serve remaining mixture in bowls.

Serves 4 to 6

Thanksgiving

34   Roasted Turkey
37   Giblet Gravy
38   Holiday Stuffing
41   Harvest Soup
42   Cranberry Sauce
45   Sweet Potato Puree
46   Pumpkin Pie

Roasted Turkey

1   12-LB TURKEY, DEFROSTED
    OLIVE OIL
1   LEMON, THINLY SLICED
1   TABLESPOON DRIED SAGE
1   TABLESPOON DRIED PARSLEY
1   TABLESPOON DRIED ROSEMARY
1   TABLESPOON DRIED THYME
    SALT AND PEPPER

1. Preheat oven to 325°F.

2. Separate skin from the breast meat, but leave it attached. Pull out neck and giblets and save for giblet gravy. Carefully rinse turkey, inside and out.

3. Mix seasonings and pulverize in a food processor. Massage oil onto turkey, under the skin, and inside the body cavity. Massage herb seasonings under the skin and inside the body cavity. Take slices of lemon and place under the skin and inside the body cavity.

4. Place a meat thermometer into the deepest part of the breast, not touching the bone. Place in a roast pan, covering loosely with foil. Baste every half hour with drippings collected in bottom of the pan.

5. After about 2 ½ hours, remove the foil. Bake the turkey for a total of about 3 ¼ to 3 ½ hours (or until thermometer reads 185°F). Remove from oven, and place turkey on a serving platter. Cover with foil and let rest for about 15 minutes to redistribute the juices.

6. Take the baking pan and deglaze with 1 cup of the giblet gravy. Once the pan is deglazed, add deglazed drippings back into the giblet gravy.

Serves 6–10

Giblet Gravy

GIBLETS AND NECK FROM TURKEY
3–5 CUPS CHICKEN BROTH
SALT AND PEPPER TO TASTE
1–2 TABLESPOONS TAPIOCA OR
POTATO STARCH
¼ CUP ICE-COLD WATER

1. In a medium sauce pan, on low heat, simmer the giblets, turkey neck, and chicken broth for about one hour (add more chicken broth gradually as it boils and evaporates off).

2. Remove the meat from the broth; let the meat cool on paper towels. Remove the meat from the neck bone and cut away any tough tissue. Cut meat into small bits and return to the broth. Use the broth to baste the turkey.

3. Once the turkey is removed from the oven and is resting, deglaze the roasting pan with the broth from the giblet gravy. Once deglazed, return to the giblet gravy.

4. Combine starch with cold water, making a slurry. Add this to the giblets and wait until the mixture boils. Cook for 1 minute or until the mixture thickens. Place in a gravy boat and serve over turkey, stuffing, and potatoes. Gravy will be lumpy due to the giblets.

Serves 6–8

Holiday Stuffing

1 CUP QUINOA
2 CUPS CHICKEN BROTH
2 LEEK STALKS, FINELY CHOPPED
1 ONION, FINELY CHOPPED
2 GRANNY SMITH APPLES, PEELED
  AND COARSELY CHOPPED
2 CUPS DRIED CRANBERRIES
1 TABLESPOON POULTRY SEASONING
  SALT AND PEPPER TO TASTE
1 CUP PISTACHIOS (OPTIONAL)

1. Preheat oven to 350°F.

2. Cook the quinoa (according to directions) with the chicken broth, adding leeks and onions to the mix.

3. Once cooked, blend quinoa mixture with the rest of the ingredients together in a large bowl.

4. Either spoon into a turkey and bake with the bird or bake in a separate casserole dish for 45 minutes at 350°F.

Serves 6–8

Harvest Soup

1 BUTTERNUT SQUASH, PEELED AND SHREDDED (IN A FOOD PROCESSOR)
2 GRANNY SMITH APPLES, PEELED AND SHREDDED
3 CARROTS, PEELED AND SHREDDED
4 CUPS WATER
¼ CUP SWEET ONION, CHOPPED FINE
1–2 TABLESPOONS FRESH GROUND GINGER
¼ TEASPOON MACE
¼ TEASPOON NUTMEG
1 TEASPOON SALT
3 TABLESPOONS MAPLE SYRUP
3 TABLESPOONS COCONUT MILK
1 CUP MILK SUBSTITUTE
2 TABLESPOONS LEMON JUICE

1. Combine all shredded/chopped vegetables/fruits in a large stock pot, add water, and let boil for about 15 minutes or until tender.

2. Add spices, syrup, and milks. Using a stick blender, puree.

3. Serve hot with crusty bread.

Serves 4–6

Tip:

You can buy pre-ground fresh ginger in jars or tubes at your local grocery store.

Cranberry Sauce

6 CUPS RAW CRANBERRIES
1 LEMON, ZEST AND JUICE
1 ORANGE, ZEST AND JUICE
1 CUP ORANGE JUICE
1 ½ CUPS SUGAR
1 TEASPOON FRESH GINGER, GRATED
½ TEASPOON CLOVE

1. Soak cranberries, sorting out rotten berries.

2. Combine ingredients in a medium sauce pan. Place over low heat and cover. Periodically stir, but simmer on low for about 2 hours, or until cranberries have popped open and released their juices.

3. Remove from pan and chill. Serve cold.

Serves 6–8

Sweet Potato Puree

1 LB SWEET POTATOES
¼ TEASPOON GROUND CLOVES
½ TEASPOON GROUND CINNAMON
¼ TEASPOON GROUND ALLSPICE
½ TEASPOON GROUND GINGER
  SALT TO TASTE
4 TABLESPOONS SAFFLOWER
  MARGARINE
¼ TO ½ CUP MILK SUBSTITUTE

1. Peel sweet potatoes and cut into large chunks. Boil until fork tender, then drain the water.

2. Using an electric mixture, whip the potatoes, adding spices, margarine, and milk substitute until mixed into the consistency of mashed potatoes.

Serves 6–10

Pumpkin Pie

1	RECIPE PIE CRUST (SEE P.207)
1	16-OZ CAN OF PUMPKIN
²/₃	CUP SUGAR
1 ½	TEASPOONS GROUND CINNAMON
½	TEASPOON FRESH GROUND GINGER
¼	TEASPOON CLOVE
¼	TEASPOON NUTMEG
3	EGGS, BEATEN
1	16-OZ CAN COCONUT MILK

1. Preheat oven to 350°F.

2. Prepare and pre-bake pie crust.

3. Blend all other ingredients together. Fill pie crust and bake for 45 minutes to an hour, or until a knife comes out clean when inserted into the center.

Serves 6–8

Sweet Potato Hash Browns

1 LB SWEET POTATOES, PEELED
1 TEASPOON GROUND NUTMEG
3 TABLESPOONS MAPLE SYRUP
1 TABLESPOON LEMON JUICE
  SALT TO TASTE
  WATER

1. Shred the peeled sweet potatoes in a food processor. Place the shredded sweet potatoes in a large frying pan and cover with water. Heat to boiling and cook for about seven minutes.

2. Once the potatoes are soft, drain off any extra water. Blend in nutmeg, salt, lemon juice, and maple syrup. Heat the mixture until it becomes just slightly crispy. Serve hot.

Serves 4–6

Easy Brussels Sprouts

4 CUPS HALVED BRUSSELS SPROUTS
⅛ CUP OLIVE OIL
1 TEASPOON GARLIC, MINCED, OR 2
  TEASPOONS HERBS DE PROVENCE
  SALT AND PEPPER TO TASTE
½ CUP PECANS (OPTIONAL)
½ MEDIUM RED ONION (OPTIONAL)

1. Preheat oven to 350°F.

2. When buying Brussels sprouts, choose fresh over frozen and pick the smaller ones. They are less likely to be bitter. Cut off the hard portion of each vegetable and remove any loose leaves. Halve each vegetable. Add oil, garlic, salt, and pepper, and mix well.

3. Spread on a baking sheet and bake for 30–35 minutes until brown.

Serves 4–6

If you do not have nut allergies, you can add pecans and red onions for a more festive version of this side dish. In case you do not have herb/grass allergies, you can substitute garlic with the herbs de Provence (savory, fennel, basil, and thyme). Whichever way you choose to prepare, this is an easy, yummy, and nutritious side dish.

Spiced Apples

4 GRANNY SMITH APPLES, PEELED, CORED, AND CUT INTO RINGS
2 TEASPOONS CINNAMON CANDY FLAVORING
½ CUP APPLE CIDER OR APPLE JUICE
2–4 DROPS RED FOOD COLORING

1. Preheat oven to 300°F.

2. Load apples into a shallow baking dish, making sure there are only a few layers of apples. Blend the cider, food coloring, and cinnamon flavoring together and pour over the apples.

3. Bake for about 10 minutes then flip the apples, ensuring even coating of the flavoring. Bake for another 10 minutes.

4. Chill and serve cold.

Serves 6–8

Cinnamon Rolls

Bread:

1 ½	CUPS RICE FLOUR
½	CUP POTATO STARCH
1	CUP TAPIOCA FLOUR
4	TEASPOONS BAKING POWDER
1	TEASPOON XANTHAN GUM
1	TEASPOON SALT
2	TABLESPOONS SUGAR
2	TABLESPOONS GROUND CINNAMON
3	LARGE EGGS
⅔	CUP CANOLA OIL
1	CUP MILK SUBSTITUTE

Filling:

5	TABLESPOONS MARGARINE, MELTED
1 ½	CUPS BROWN SUGAR
4	TABLESPOONS GROUND CINNAMON

1. Preheat oven to 350°F.

2. Mix the dry ingredients well then add the wet ingredients. Mix well in a large bowl. The texture should be like biscuit dough.

3. Spray two long (24") pieces of plastic wrap with Pam. Scoop half of the dough onto one piece of greased plastic wrap, cover with the other piece, and grease side down. With your hands slowly spread the dough to the edges of the plastic wrap until the dough is about ¼-inch thick. Remove the top layer of plastic wrap.

4. Spread on the melted margarine and then the brown sugar/cinnamon mixture until the entire dough is coated. Pull up on one side of the plastic wrap, coaxing the dough to start rolling, and continue until the entire dough is in a log formation.

5. Cut the log into 1- to 2-inch pieces and place them into a large, greased baking dish. Repeat with the remaining dough. With any leftover brown sugar/cinnamon mixture, top the finished rolls.

6. Bake for 40 minutes until golden brown.

Serves 8–12

CHAPTER SIX:

Soups

60   Bok Choy Soup
63   Bosnian Wedding Soup
64   Chicken Soup with Dumplings
67   Cream of Broccoli Soup
68   Cream of Mushroom Soup
71   Garlic Ginger Soup
72   Seafood Chowder

Bok Choy Soup

2 CUPS BOK CHOY, WHITES COARSELY
    CHOPPED, GREENS CHIFFONADE
3 STALKS GREEN ONION, COARSELY
    CHOPPED
1 TEASPOON GARLIC, MINCED
1 CUP MUSHROOMS, CHOPPED
1 CUP SHREDDED CARROTS
4 CUPS CHICKEN STOCK
½ CUP GROUND TURKEY, BROWNED
1 TEASPOON POULTRY SEASONING
½ TEASPOON DRIED CILANTRO
1 TABLESPOON LEMON JUICE
    SALT AND PEPPER TO TASTE

1. Stir fry vegetables until
   bok choy begins to wilt
   and mushrooms get soft.
   Add turkey and stock, and
   bring to a boil.

2. Add seasoning, lemon
   juice, and then serve.

Serves 4–6

Hot Tip:

Save your leftover meat carcasses (turkey, chicken, beef, pork bones). You can make an easy stock from them. In a large stock pot, place the bones, large chunks of carrots, onions, celery, or leeks, and a bundle of fresh herbs, and add enough water to cover the bones. Boil on a slow simmer for about 2 to 3 hours. Remove and discard the bones and vegetables. Skim the fat off the top. Place 1 cup of the finished stock in disposable plastic containers and freeze. Use the 1 cup portions of stock to add to other soups or sauce bases. This not only saves money (not having to pay for canned stock) but it's also a lot healthier than the store-bought stocks. You can add as much salt and pepper as you like.

Bosnian Wedding Soup

Soup

- 4 CUPS VEGETABLE STOCK
- 2 TABLESPOONS DRIED, UNSEASONED VEGETABLE SOUP MIX
  SALT AND PEPPER
- 1 TEASPOON FRESH PARSLEY, FINELY CHOPPED

Dumplings

- 1 CUP CREAM OF RICE CEREAL
- ¼ TEASPOON SALT
- 1 EGG, BEATEN
- ¼ CUP MILK SUBSTITUTE ADDED 1 TABLESPOON AT A TIME

1. Combine chicken stock, dried vegetables, and salt and pepper to taste. Heat until boiling. Turn down heat and let simmer.

2. While the soup is heating, mix dry ingredients for the dumplings. Add egg and milk 1 tablespoon at a time and mix with dry ingredients. The consistency of the batter should be that of coarse meal. If it is too soft, you added too much milk substitute.

3. Using a teaspoon, drop batter into the simmering soup. Let the dumplings cook for about 15 minutes at a steady simmer.

4. Add parsley just before serving.

Serves 4

Chicken Soup with Dumplings

Soup

4 BONELESS, SKINLESS CHICKEN BREASTS
2 CARROTS
2 STALKS CELERY
½ CUP RED ONION, DICED
1 CLOVE OF GARLIC, MINCED
1 CUP MUSHROOMS, SLICED
2 TABLESPOONS OLIVE OIL
6 CUPS CHICKEN STOCK
  SALT AND PEPPER
1 TEASPOON FRESH PARSLEY, FINELY CHOPPED
1 TEASPOON FRESH TARRAGON, FINELY CHOPPED

Dumplings

1 CUP FLOUR MIXTURE (SEE P. 10)
2 TEASPOONS BAKING POWDER
¼ TEASPOON SALT
¼ TEASPOON OREGANO
1 EGG, BEATEN
¼ CUP MILK SUBSTITUTE

1. Dice chicken and vegetables. Heat oil in a large soup pan and sweat the onions and garlic. Add mushrooms and stir until they begin to weep their juices. Add chicken and cook until chicken appears white.

2. Add chicken stock and salt and pepper to taste. Heat until boiling. Turn down heat and let simmer.

3. While soup is heating, mix the dry ingredients for the dumplings. Add egg and milk; mix with the dry ingredients. Drop batter into the simmering soup, about ping-pong-ball sized. Let cook for about 15 minutes at a steady simmer.

4. Add parsley and tarragon just before serving.

Serves 6

Cream of Broccoli Soup

20 OZ FROZEN, CHOPPED BROCCOLI,
OR 2 FULL HEADS FRESH BROCCOLI
½ CUP ONION, CHOPPED
3   CUPS CHICKEN BROTH
2   TABLESPOONS FLOUR MIXTURE (SEE
P. 10)
2   TABLESPOONS OLIVE OIL
1   TEASPOON SALT
½ TEASPOON MACE
1   16-OZ CAN COCONUT MILK
1   CUP MILK SUBSTITUTE (RICE MILK
OR SOY MILK)
PEPPER TO TASTE

1. Combine onion, broccoli, and broth in a stock pot. Simmer for about 10 minutes until broccoli is tender. Using a stick blender, or in small batches in a food processer, blend mixture until almost smooth.

2. In another pot, make a roux with an oil and flour mixture, and slowly stir in milks to make a cream sauce. Add the cream sauce to the broccoli puree in the stock pot and heat the entire soup over medium heat until it bubbles, stirring often.

Serves 4–6

Cream of Mushroom Soup

3 CUPS FRESH MUSHROOMS, CHOPPED (EQUAL PARTS WHITE MUSHROOMS, CRIMINI MUSHROOMS, OYSTER MUSHROOMS, OR PORTOBELLO MUSHROOMS)

3 SCALLIONS, FINELY CHOPPED

3 CLOVES OF GARLIC, SMASHED AND CHOPPED

3 TABLESPOONS OLIVE OIL + 2 TABLESPOONS OLIVE OIL FOR LATER

2 TABLESPOONS FLOUR (WHEAT, RICE, POTATO, RYE, OR TAPIOCA)

1 CUP CHICKEN BROTH

½ CUP COCONUT MILK

2 ½ CUPS MILK SUBSTITUTE

½ CUP WHITE WINE

SALT AND PEPPER TO TASTE

1 TEASPOON FRESH PARSLEY, CHOPPED

½ TEASPOON EACH: MARJORAM, OREGANO, AND ROSEMARY, GROUND FINE

½ CUP POTATO FLAKES

1. In a stock pot, fry mushrooms, scallions, and garlic in 3 tablespoons olive oil until juicy. Add wine and set aside.

2. In a medium sauce pan, heat up remaining 2 tablespoons olive oil and add flour, making a roux.

3. Blend together milk, coconut milk, and chicken broth. Slowly add this liquid into the roux, blending out any lumps. The mix will thicken quickly.

4. Add the cream sauce to the mushroom mix, potato flakes, and spices. Heat to simmering for about 10 minutes. Serve with crusty bread.

Serves 4–6

Garlic Ginger Soup

1 TABLESPOON SAFFLOWER
MARGARINE

2 TEASPOONS GARLIC, MINCED, OR
GARLIC PASTE

2 TEASPOONS GRATED GINGER ROOT
OR GINGER PASTE

2 TEASPOONS LEMONGRASS
SEASONING

4 CUPS CHICKEN STOCK

3 TABLESPOONS DRIED, UNSEASONED
VEGETABLE SOUP MIX (SOLD IN THE
PRODUCE DEPARTMENT)

½ CUP THIN RICE NOODLES, CRUSHED
(YOU CAN ADD MORE TO ADJUST TO
YOUR LIKING)
LEMON JUICE OR LIME JUICE
TO TASTE

1. Fry garlic and ginger in margarine until brown.

2. Add chicken stock and unseasoned vegetable soup mix, and bring to a boil. Add noodles by crushing them with your fingers. Add lemongrass seasoning.

3. Boil noodles for 5 minutes then remove from the stove and let it sit for another 10 minutes.

4. Serve into bowls and squeeze lemon or lime juice to taste.

Serves 4

Seafood Chowder

12 SMALL RED POTATOES, COARSELY
    CHOPPED WITH SKINS ON

4 STRIPS BACON, RESERVE 2
    TABLESPOONS BACON FAT

¼ CUP RED ONION, FINELY CHOPPED

1 CUP CHICKEN STOCK

2 TABLESPOONS FLOUR (ANY TYPE
    WILL DO)

3 CUPS MILK SUBSTITUTE

½ CUP COCONUT MILK

2 10-OZ CANS OF WHOLE CLAMS WITH
    THEIR JUICE (OR 2 CUPS COOKED
    FISH, BROKEN TO SMALL PIECES)

½ CUP FROZEN CORN (OPTIONAL)

1 TEASPOON LEMON JUICE

2 TEASPOONS SALT

1 TEASPOON PEPPER

¼ TEASPOON DRIED DILL

¼ TEASPOON MARJORAM

¼ TEASPOON TARRAGON

⅛ TEASPOON MACE

1. Boil chopped potatoes until fork tender, drain, and separate into halves. Mash half of the potatoes.

2. Fry bacon until crisp, reserving 2 tablespoons of bacon fat. Drain bacon on paper towels.

3. Fry onions in bacon fat until translucent. Add flour and create a roux. Slowly add chicken stock and milk (alternating), stirring out any lumps. The mixture should be creamy and smooth.

4. Add coconut milk, clams, and juice and/or fish, lemon juice, corn, potatoes (mashed and cubed), and seasonings. Bring to a slow boil over medium heat.

5. Serve hot. Note: It tastes even better the next day.

Serves 4–6

CHAPTER SEVEN

Appetizers

76	Bread Sticks
79	Creamy White Bean Dip
80	Flat Bread
83	Greek Bok Choy Topper
84	Guacamole
87	Puffed Flat Bread
88	Stuffed Mushrooms

The Food Allergy Cookbook

Bread Sticks

¼ OZ ACTIVE DRY YEAST
1 CUP WARM WATER
⅛ CUP SUGAR
¼ CUP OIL
1 TEASPOON SALT
1 EGG
3 CUPS FLOUR MIXTURE (SEE P.10)
½ CUP GLUTINOUS RICE FLOUR

For garnish
1 EGG YOLK
⅛ CUP SWEET RICE FLOUR
⅛ CUP COLD WATER
2 TABLESPOONS SALT

1. Preheat oven to 425°F.

2. In a mixing bowl, dissolve yeast in warm water. Add oil and sugar and let stand for 5 minutes.

3. Add salt, flour, and one egg to form soft dough. Turn onto a floured surface; knead until smooth and elastic. Do not let the dough rise. Divide dough into 20–24 equal pieces and shape each into a log 6–8 inches long. Place logs on greased baking sheets and let rest for 10 minutes.

4. Add a couple tablespoons of water to the remaining egg yolk then beat with the fork until combined. Use a pastry brush to brush egg wash on each log.

5. Combine ⅛ cup sweet rice flour, 2 tablespoons salt, and ⅛ cup cold water to form batter. The batter should be the consistency of a pancake mix.

6. Drizzle the batter over the bread sticks then bake them for 10–12 minutes. Note: bread sticks will never be golden brown in color.

Makes 20–24 bread sticks

Creamy White Bean Dip

1   15-OZ CAN WHITE BEANS
2   CLOVES ROASTED GARLIC,
    CRUSHED
2   TABLESPOONS FRESH PARSLEY,
    PLUS SOME FOR GARNISH
    SALT AND PEPPER TO TASTE
1   15-OZ CAN ARTICHOKE BOTTOMS
¼   CUP PINE NUTS (OPTIONAL)
2–5 DROPS TABASCO SAUCE
    PAPRIKA

1. Drain and rinse the beans and artichokes. Combine all ingredients into a food processor and puree until very smooth.

2. Place in a decorative bowl and garnish with extra parsley and paprika.

3. Serve with rice crackers, chopped vegetables, or chips.

Serves 6–10

Hot Tip:

When attending a potluck-style dinner, try to bring something that you can eat *and* that everyone will enjoy. Also, be sure to eat something light before going to the potluck as it is sometimes very risky to eat food prepared by others (you don't know what allergens might be included). Use the potluck as an opportunity to educate others about your allergies and to introduce them to some delicious, allergen-free dishes.

Flat Bread

3 CUPS FLOUR MIXTURE (SEE P.10)
1 TABLESPOON SUGAR
1 TEASPOON SALT
2 TEASPOONS BAKING POWDER
½ CUP WARM MILK SUBSTITUTE
2 TABLESPOONS OIL
¾ CUP WARM WATER

1. Mix all of the ingredients to form soft but non-sticky dough.

2. Divide dough into 4 pieces. Roll each piece into a ball then flatten into a disk. Brush the disk of dough with oil on both sides and place in between two sheets of parchment paper. The dough should be covered and set aside for 30 minutes.

3. Place a large frying pan or a griddle over a medium-high heat. Do not grease the pan. Wait till the pan warms up then roll the dough disks, one by one, into an 8-inch circle using a rolling pin.

4. Remove the top sheet of the parchment paper and slide the rolling pin under the bottom sheet of the paper. Transfer the dough into the frying pan and peel off the remaining sheet of parchment paper. Wait till the dough starts to bubble then flip it. The bread is done when brown spots are formed on its surface.

5. Transfer the cooked bread piece to a plate and cover to keep warm until all pieces are done.

Serves 4

Greek Bok Choy Topper

1   LB GROUND LAMB
2   TABLESPOONS OLIVE OIL
1   CLOVE OF GARLIC, MINCED
1   SHALLOT, MINCED
½   TEASPOON DRIED MINT
2   LARGE HEADS OF BOK CHOY, CUT
    INTO LARGE PIECES
¼   CUP PINE NUTS (OPTIONAL)

1. In a large skillet, brown the ground lamb and drain off the fat, then set it aside.

2. Using the same skillet, heat olive oil then fry the garlic and shallot until translucent. Wilt the bok choy in the garlic/shallot mixture. Add pine nuts if you like.

3. Return the ground lamb to the pan, along with the bok choy. Garnish with dried mint.

4. Serve on toast points, as a pizza topper, or as a side dish.

Serves 4

Guacamole

2 AVOCADOS
1 TABLESPOON GARLIC, MINCED
1 ½ TEASPOONS FRESH CILANTRO, CHOPPED
¼ CUP RED ONION, CHOPPED
¼ CUP TOMATO, CHOPPED AND SEEDED
JUICE FROM ONE LIME
4 SHOTS TABASCO SAUCE
1 HOT PEPPER, CHOPPED AND SEEDED (OPTIONAL)

1. Cut avocados lengthwise, saving the pits. Scoop out the meat and mash in a bowl.

2. Add other ingredients and blend together. Mixture should be lumpy. Store in an airtight bowl with the avocado pits in with the guacamole (it will keep the guacamole from browning).

3. Serve with tortilla chips, rice chips, or slather on a sandwich.

Puffed Flat Bread

¼ OZ ACTIVE DRY YEAST
1 CUP WARM WATER
⅛ CUP SUGAR
¼ CUP OLIVE OIL
1 TEASPOON SALT
3 CUPS FLOUR MIXTURE (SEE P.10)
½ CUP GLUTINOUS FLOUR (RICE,
   SPELT, OAT, RYE, ETC.)

1. In a mixing bowl, dissolve yeast in warm water. Add oil and sugar and let stand for 5 minutes.

2. Add salt and flour to form a soft dough. Knead the dough until smooth and elastic. Transfer it into a greased bowl; cover and let sit for an hour or until doubled in size.

3. Divide dough into 8 equal pieces. Working with one piece of dough at a time on a lightly floured surface, roll into a circle ¼-inch in thickness. Cut the dough in quarters.

4. Heat a 10-inch skillet over medium heat. Add enough oil to cover the bottom of the skillet then fry the dough. When the pieces start to bubble up, turn them and fry the other side.

Serves 8

Stuffed Mushrooms

12 LARGE PORCINI OR WHITE
   MUSHROOMS
2 TABLESPOONS OLIVE OIL
1 CLOVE GARLIC, MINCED
¼ CUP ONION, FINELY CHOPPED
¼ CUP CRUSHED RICE CRACKERS OR
   "BREAD" CRUMBS
   SALT AND PEPPER TO TASTE

1. Preheat oven to 350°F.

2. Clean mushrooms and separate stems from the caps. Clean out the gills. Finely chop mushroom stems and gills.

3. Using a medium pan, heat olive oil. Add garlic and onion and stir fry until translucent. Add mushroom stems. Cook until mushroom mixture begins to weep. Add seasoning and crackers.

4. Pack the mixture into the mushroom caps, packing fairly firm. Place mushroom caps in an ovenproof baking dish and bake for about 20 minutes or until caps are fork tender.

5. Serve hot.

Serves 4

*Optional add-ins:

Crab

Smoked Salmon

CHAPTER EIGHT

Salads and Side Dishes

92	Acorn Squash
95	Applesauce
96	Broccoli Salad
99	Carrot Salad
100	Korn Bread
103	Mexican Yellow Rice
104	Pasta Salad
107	Potato Ravioli
108	Quirky Coleslaw
111	Risotto

Acorn Squash

1 ACORN SQUASH
½–1 CUP WATER
1 TEASPOON FRESHLY GRATED
GINGER

Filling
¼ CUP BROWN SUGAR
½ TEASPOON GROUND CINNAMON
¼ TEASPOON CLOVES
¼ TEASPOON NUTMEG
1 TEASPOON LEMON JUICE
2 TABLESPOONS MARGARINE
SALT

1. Preheat oven to 350°F.

2. Halve and clean the acorn squash of its seeds. Poke holes in the squash meat and place face down in a shallow, microwave/ovenproof dish. Add water and ginger, mixing the ginger so it's evenly distributed in the water.

3. Heat on high in the microwave for about 10 minutes or until the squash is fork tender. Pour off water.

4. Place the squash face up in the same dish. Combine ingredients for the filling, excluding the salt. Sprinkle the squash with salt and fill the bowls of the squash with the filling, splitting it evenly between the two halves. Top with a pat of margarine.

5. Bake in the oven for about 5 minutes or until the sugar has melted.

Serves 2

Applesauce

1 CUP CIDER
2 TABLESPOONS LEMON JUICE
7 GRANNY SMITH APPLES, COARSELY
  CHOPPED WITH SKINS ON
1 CUP SUGAR
1 TABLESPOON GROUND CINNAMON

1. Acidulate the cut apples with lemon juice.

2. Place all ingredients in a large stock pot and slowly simmer (on low) until apples are soft.

3. Using a stick blender, puree the mixture.

4. Serve hot or cold. Will store refrigerated for about 2 weeks.

Serves 8–12

> ### *Hot Tip:*
> Applesauce is a great substitute for oils in baked goods.

Broccoli Salad

2   CUPS BROCCOLI FLORETS, FINELY CUT TO SMALLEST STEMS

1   TABLESPOON DRIED ONION FLAKES

¼   CUP SALTED SUNFLOWER SEEDS

¼   CUP FRIED BACON BITS

¼   CUP DRIED RAISINS

½   CUP SAFFLOWER/CANOLA OR OLIVE OIL MAYO

2   TABLESPOONS APPLE CIDER VINEGAR

1–2   TABLESPOONS HONEY, RICE SYRUP, OR SUGAR

1. In a pan fry the bacon until crisp. Place the bacon on a paper towel to drain the fat.

2. In a bowl mix the mayo, apple cider vinegar, and sweetener. If it is too tart for your taste add more sweetener.

3. Mix all of the ingredients and let the salad sit for at least 30 minutes before serving.

Serves 4–6

Carrot Salad

4–5 CUPS SHREDDED CARROTS
1 CUP RAISINS
1 TABLESPOON GROUND CINNAMON
½ TEASPOON SALT
2 TABLESPOONS MAPLE SYRUP

1. Mix ingredients in a large bowl. Serve cold.

Serves about 12

Hot Tip:

Lots of kids don't like to eat vegetables so try to sneak them into their diet by including shredded carrots, zucchini, and the like in spaghetti sauce or pizza sauce.

Korn Bread

1 CUP CREAM OF RICE CEREAL
½ CUP FLOUR MIXTURE (SEE P.10)
½ CUP VEGETABLE OIL
½ CUP MILK SUBSTITUTE
½ CUP SPARKLING WATER
3 TEASPOONS BAKING POWDER
4 EGGS
1 TABLESPOON PLAIN YOGURT
  (OPTIONAL)
¾ CUP RAISINS
1 TABLESPOON CARAWAY SEEDS
  SALT AND SUGAR TO TASTE

1. Preheat oven to 350°F.

2. Combine all the dry ingredients and set aside. In a separate bowl, combine all the wet ingredients except for sparkling water.

3. Mix wet and dry ingredients using hand whisk. Add raisins and caraway seeds. Add sparkling water.

4. Pour into a greased 9 x 13 pan and bake 30–40 minutes.

Serves 6–8

Mexican Yellow Rice

3	TABLESPOONS OLIVE OIL
1	MEDIUM ONION, FINELY CHOPPED
2 ½	TEASPOONS GARLIC, FINELY CHOPPED
½	TEASPOON TURMERIC
½	TEASPOON CAYENNE PEPPER
½	TEASPOON DRIED CILANTRO
1	CUP RICE, UNCOOKED
2	CUPS BEEF OR CHICKEN BROTH

1. Fry onion and garlic in oil until browned.

2. Add turmeric, cayenne pepper, and rice. Stir the rice until it is coated with oil and spices. It should be glossy.

3. Add broth and let it simmer for 15 minutes. Add cilantro and let it simmer for another 5 minutes. Serve.

Serves 4–6

Pasta Salad

2 CUPS GLUTEN-FREE PASTA, COOKED
1 RED ONION, DICED
1 GREEN OR RED PEPPER, DICED
1 3-OZ CAN TUNA
2 TABLESPOONS FRESH BASIL, FINELY
   CHOPPED
   SALT AND PEPPER TO TASTE
4 TABLESPOONS OLIVE OIL
1 TABLESPOON BALSAMIC VINEGAR
1 TEASPOON SUGAR

1. Mix pasta, vegetables, and fish in a large bowl. Season to taste.

2. Using a whisk, start mixing the olive oil, slowly adding vinegar and sugar.

3. Add dressing to the pasta. Garnish with fresh basil. Serve cold.

Serves 4–6

Potato Ravioli

RAVIOLI DOUGH
1   LB POTATOES, DICED
3   SMALL EGG YOLKS
3   TABLESPOONS OIL
1 ½ CUPS FLOUR MIXTURE (SEE P.10)
¼   CUP OIL FOR FRYING
     SHREDDED PARSLEY LEAVES FOR
     GARNISH

Filling
1   TABLESPOON OLIVE OIL
1   CUP GROUND MEAT (TURKEY, BEEF,
     PORK)
1   SMALL ONION, DICED
1   GARLIC CLOVE, CRUSHED
½   CUP BEEF STOCK
2   MEDIUM TOMATOES, DICED
2   TEASPOONS FRESH PARSLEY,
     CHOPPED
     SALT AND PEPPER

1. In a pan, fry the meat for 3–4 minutes, breaking it up with the spoon. Add onion and garlic and cook for an additional 2–3 minutes, or until the onion has softened.

2. Stir in the flour, beef stock, tomatoes, and parsley and season to taste with salt and pepper. Cook the mixture over low heat for 20 minutes. Remove from the heat and leave to cool.

3. Cook the potatoes in a pan of boiling water. Mash the cooked potatoes and add salt and pepper to taste then blend in the egg yolks and oil. Stir in the flour and mix to form dough. Divide the dough into 24 pieces and shape pieces into balls. Place each ball between two sheets of plastic wrap and pat or roll into a flat round.

4. Spoon some filling onto one side of each round and fold the dough over. Using your fingers pinch the edges to seal in the filling.

5. In a frying pan heat up ¼ cup oil. Cook ravioli until golden on each side, about 6–8 minutes.

6. Serve hot, garnished with parsley.

Serves 4–6

Quirky Coleslaw

Salad

1 BAG SHREDDED CABBAGE, OR
  SHRED 1 HEAD OF CABBAGE FINELY
½ CUP DRIED FRUIT (RAISINS,
  PINEAPPLE, CRANBERRIES,
  CURRENTS, ETC.)
½ CUP NUTS, FINELY CHOPPED
  (OPTIONAL)

Dressing

½ CUP MAYONNAISE
1 TABLESPOON VINEGAR
2 TEASPOONS SUGAR
1 TABLESPOON POPPY SEEDS
½ TEASPOON CELERY SALT

1. Mix together salad ingredients.

2. Whip dressing and blend with salad until everything is evenly coated with the dressing.

3. Serve cold.

Serves 8–10

Hot Tip:

When you're on a road trip, you will find most drive-thru restaurants can be "iffy" for folks with food allergies. Keep a steady supply of trail mix, protein bars, or dried fruit with you in case you get hungry and cannot find a place to stop.

Risotto

2	TABLESPOONS OLIVE OIL
¼	CUP ONION, FINELY CHOPPED
2	CLOVES GARLIC, MINCED
1	CUP MUSHROOMS, FINELY CHOPPED
⅓	CUP SMOKED FISH (EG. SALMON)
1 ½	CUPS CHICKEN STOCK
1	CUP RISOTTO (WASHED)/ARBORIO RICE
1	TEASPOON FRESH TARRAGON, FINELY CHOPPED
2	TEASPOONS FRESH PARSLEY, FINELY CHOPPED

1. In a large, deep fry pan sweat the olive oil with onion, garlic, and mushrooms.

2. Add the risotto and fry until just beginning to smell nutty. Slowly add a little stock, stirring frequently. Cover in between stirs. Continue adding stock at regular intervals after risotto has absorbed previous liquid.

3. Once risotto has absorbed all liquid, add herbs and serve.

Serves 4–6

CHAPTER NINE

Entrees

114	Apple Stuffed Pork Loin
117	Baked Chicken
118	Barbecue Chicken Legs
121	Barbecue Sauce
122	Barbecued Sloppy Joes
125	Basic Crepes
126	Blood Orange Rockfish
129	Chicken Crepes
130	Chicken Pot Pie
133	Cream Dried Beef on Toast
134	Herbed Pizza Crust
137	Lamb Patties
138	Mustard Glazed Salmon
141	Pizza Crust
142	Salmon with Minty Mustard
145	Seafood Loaf
146	Shepherd's Pie
149	Steak with Mushrooms
150	Stuffed Peppers Bosnian Style
153	Sweet Ham Bake
154	Vegetarian Stuffed Peppers

Apple Stuffed Pork Loin

2   PORK LOINS
1   LARGE TART APPLE, DICED
1   TABLESPOON FRESHLY GROUND
    GINGER
1   SHALLOT, DICED
    OLIVE OIL
4   TABLESPOONS PLUM BUTTER
    OR PRESERVES
    SALT AND PEPPER TO TASTE

1. Preheat oven to 350°F.

2. Mix the diced apple with the ginger, plum butter, and shallots.

3. Butterfly open the pork loins to create space for stuffing. Salt and pepper the loin, then massage with oil. Stuff the loin with the apple mixture, reserving about ¼ for the top. Fold the top half of the loin over, and top with the remainder of the apple mixture.

4. Bake for about 20 minutes, or until the loin reaches an internal temperature of 125°F.

Serves 4

Baked Chicken

4   SKINLESS, BONELESS CHICKEN
      BREASTS
3–4 TABLESPOONS DIJON MUSTARD
      PAM OR OTHER NON-STICK SPRAY
½   CUP HONEY

1. Preheat oven to 350°F.

2. Wash and pat dry the chicken. Trim off excess fat or non-edible tissue. Tenderize chicken breasts with a mallet in between sheets of wax paper.

3. Spread about a tablespoon of mustard on each breast, then roll the breast, securing it with toothpicks. Drizzle on honey.

4. Bake for about 25 minutes (until cooked).

Serves 4

Hot Tip:

If you are traveling and need to eat out in restaurants, try creating "allergy alert cards" on standard-sized business cards. This way, you can detail what foods you need to avoid. Give these to the waiter so they can be sure to explain to the chef your dietary needs. If you're traveling in a foreign country, have these cards translated into the official language of the country you'll be visiting. It will save you lots of stomach aches!

The Food Allergy Cookbook

Barbecue Chicken Legs

8   CHICKEN DRUMSTICKS
2   CUPS BARBECUE SAUCE
    SALT AND PEPPER TO TASTE

1. Preheat oven to 375°F.

2. Clean the chicken and remove all skins. Salt and pepper then soak the chicken in 1 ½ cups of barbecue sauce.

3. Heat a stovetop grill pan on medium heat and spray lightly with oil or Pam. Once the pan is hot, brown the chicken on each side.

4. Place the seared chicken into a greased baking pan and bake for about 30 minutes or until the chicken reaches an internal temperature of 165°F.

5. Reapply some of the remaining barbecue sauce and keep some for dipping.

Serves 4

Barbecue Sauce

2 TABLESPOONS OIL
1 TEASPOON GARLIC, MINCED
¼ CUP ONION, CHOPPED
⅓ CUP KETCHUP
⅓ CUP MOLASSES
⅓ CUP BROWN SUGAR
3 TABLESPOONS VINEGAR
½ TEASPOON CLOVES
1 TEASPOON MUSTARD POWDER
10 SHOTS TABASCO SAUCE OR
    PEPPER SAUCE

1. Mix together all ingredients in a medium sauce pan.

2. Stir until all ingredients are mixed and heated through. Simmer until reduced by a third.

3. Use as a topping on ribs, chicken, beef, and the like.

Makes about 1 cup of sauce

Barbecued Sloppy Joes

1 LB GROUND MEAT (BEEF, PORK, TURKEY)
¼ CUP BARBECUE SAUCE
GLUTEN FREE BURGER ROLLS OR BREAD

1. Brown the meat, then drain off any fat.

2. Add the barbecue sauce and mix until coated and heated through.

3. Fill burger rolls and serve.

Serves 4

Basic Crepes

1 ½   CUPS MILK SUBSTITUTE
2   TABLESPOONS OIL
3   EGGS
1 ½   CUPS FLOUR MIXTURE (SEE P.10)
⅛   TEASPOON SALT

1. Blend all ingredients in a blender.

2. One method of making crepes is with a crepe maker. Using a paper towel dipped in oil, grease the crepe maker. Pour batter into a shallow plate and make crepes. Next, invert the crepe maker into the batter, making sure there is an even coat of batter on the crepe maker. Turn when the batter begins to bubble (about 30 seconds). Remove the crepe after about 20 seconds.

3. The other method is to spoon about ¼ cup of crepe batter into a shallow pan that is well heated. Turn the pan so that the batter covers the entire pan. Turn again after about 30 seconds and heat through on the other side.

4. Fill with whatever filling you desire.

Makes about 2 dozen crepes

Variations on the Basic Recipe
DESSERT CREPES

1. Basic crepe recipe plus ¼ cup sugar, 1 ½ teaspoon vanilla, and if desired, 2 tablespoons unsweetened cocoa powder.

HERB CREPES

1. Basic crepe recipe plus 1 teaspoon each of oregano, basil, thyme, parsley, and marjoram.

Blood Orange Rockfish

4   FRESH ROCKFISH FILLETS
     (HALIBUT OR COD IS A NICE
     SUBSTITUTE)
2   SHALLOTS, DICED
2   CARROTS, DICED
2   CUPS BROWN RICE, COOKED
2   BLOOD ORANGES
1   LEMON
1   TABLESPOON HONEY
6–10 SAFFRON THREADS
1–2 BOK CHOY HEADS
     SALT AND PEPPER TO TASTE
     OLIVE OIL

1. Zest oranges and lemon and set aside.

2. Juice the lemon and oranges and add zest and honey to the juice. Heat the juice (in the microwave for about 1 minute) until scalding. Add the saffron and let the saffron bloom in the hot juice; set aside.

3. Split the bok choy, separating the white from the greens. Dice the whites of the bok choy and chiffonade the greens.

4. In a large wok or skillet, heat enough olive oil to coat the pan. Add shallots, carrots, and whites of bok choy, stirring constantly for about 5 minutes or until fork tender. Add rice and salt and pepper to taste.

5. Just before removing the rice mixture from the heat, add the bok choy greens. Sauté the greens until just wilting. Remove the entire mixture from heat and set it aside.

6. Salt and pepper the fish fillets. In another large pan, heat enough olive oil to coat the pan. Gently add the fillets and pour citrus juice into the pan. Poach the fish in the citrus/saffron juice for about 3 minutes on each side, or until fish begins to separate.

7. Plate presentation should be rice mixture with the fish fillet on top and the citrus sauce drizzled down across the fish.

Serves 4–6

Chicken Crepes

2   DOZEN BASIC OR HERB CREPES
    (SEE P. 125)
2   CUPS CHICKEN, CHOPPED
    AND COOKED
2   TABLESPOONS RICE FLOUR
4   TABLESPOONS OLIVE OIL
¼   TEASPOON POULTRY SEASONING
¼   TEASPOON GARLIC, MINCED
1   CUP CHICKEN STOCK
¼   CUP CARROTS, CHOPPED
¼   CUP PEAS (FRESH OR FROZEN)
    SALT AND PEPPER TO TASTE

1. Brown chicken in 2 tablespoons oil then remove the chicken from the pan and set aside.

2. With remaining oil create a roux with the olive oil and flour. Slowly add the chicken stock until there is a thick sauce. Add salt and pepper, vegetables, and chicken seasonings.

3. Cook for about 15 minutes over medium heat, adding more chicken stock if the sauce becomes too thick.

4. Spoon finished sauce over crepes and fold into thirds, like a burrito.

Serves 4

Chicken Pot Pie

Filling

2 ½	LBS CHICKEN
1	ONION, HALVED
1	STALK CELERY, CUT INTO PIECES
1	CUP CARROTS, CHOPPED
1	LARGE POTATO, COOKED AND CUBED
1	PARSLEY ROOT
¼	CUP FRESH PARSLEY, CHOPPED
½	CUP FROZEN PEAS
½	TEASPOON SALT

Sauce

½	CUP SWEET RICE FLOUR
1	CUP VEGETABLE BROTH
1	CUP CHICKEN BROTH
1	CUP COCONUT MILK

Pie Pastry for 4 miniature pie pans (5-inch)

½	CUP TAPIOCA STARCH
½	CUP POTATO STARCH
½	CUP GLUTINOUS RICE FLOUR
¾	CUP SWEET RICE FOUR
1	TEASPOON XANTHAN GUM
½	TEASPOON SALT
	DASH OF SUGAR

Shortening Mix

1	CUP PALM SEED SHORTENING	6	TEASPOONS COLD WATER
¼	TEASPOON BUTTER EXTRACT	1	EGG YOLK
1	EGG	6	TABLESPOONS COLD WATER
1	TABLESPOON RICE VINEGAR		

1. Preheat oven to 400°F.

2. Combine meat and vegetables into a 2-quart pot. Add salt, cover with water, and bring to a boil. Reduce heat and simmer until meat is cooked and vegetables are tender, about 1 hour. Let it cool.

3. Strain broth and reserve 2 cups of it. Chop meat and vegetables into cubes. In a separate pot combine the ingredients for the sauce and bring to boil. Stir in meat and vegetables; set aside to cool.

4. To make crusts, blend the dry ingredients together then cut in the shortening mix. Work the dough until it starts to resemble lumps like soft cookie dough.

5. Beat the eggs using a fork; add vinegar and ice water. Stir into the flour mixture and knead using your

fingers. The dough will start off very soft, but as you knead it you will notice how quickly the liquid is absorbed and the dough starts to separate from the walls of the bowl. Divide into 8 equal parts and store in the refrigerator no longer than 15 minutes.

6. Place a ball of dough in between two sheets of plastic wrap and roll into a 6 ½-inch circle. Remove the top sheet of plastic wrap and put a 5-inch miniature pie pan on top of it. Slide your hand under the bottom sheet of plastic wrap and invert the pie pan and the dough. While the plastic wrap is still on the dough, move the dough so it covers the inside and the sides of the pan evenly. Remove the plastic wrap and fill the pan with the filling.

7. Roll out the top layer of the pie crust to a 6-inch circle, flute the edges, and make cuts in the dough to let the steam escape during baking.

8. Combine one whole egg and one tablespoon of water; beat with the fork. Using a pastry brush, put egg wash on each pie.

9. Bake for 20 minutes or until golden brown.

Serves 4

Cream Dried Beef on Toast

2	TABLESPOONS OLIVE OIL
2	PACKAGES PROCESSED SANDWICH BEEF, CUT UP INTO 1-INCH SQUARES
2	TABLESPOONS RICE FLOUR
1 ½	CUPS MILK SUBSTITUTE
	SALT AND PEPPER TO TASTE
4	SLICES OF TOAST
2	EGGS, HARDBOILED AND DICED

1. Heat oil in a large pan.

2. Fry beef in oil until edges curl. Add flour and mix well. Slowly add milk until a thick sauce is made. Add salt and pepper to taste.

3. Spoon mixture over toast and top with eggs.

Serves 4

Herbed Pizza Crust

2 CUPS FLOUR MIXTURE (SEE P.10)

2 TEASPOONS GUAR OR XANTHAN GUM

1 PACKAGE (¾ OZ) RAPID RISE DRY YEAST

2 TEASPOONS BAKING POWDER

1 TABLESPOON DRIED OREGANO FLAKES

1 TABLESPOON ITALIAN SEASONING

1 CUP WARM WATER (ADD MORE WATER BY THE TABLESPOON IF NEEDED)

1 TABLESPOON SUGAR

1 TEASPOON SALT

1 TABLESPOON OLIVE OIL

1 TEASPOON VINEGAR

1 EGG

2 TABLESPOONS EXTRA RICH NON-DAIRY CREAMER (WATCH FOR CASEIN CONTENT) (OPTIONAL)

1. Preheat oven to 425°F.

2. Combine all of the above ingredients and beat with an electric mixer until well combined.

3. Place in the mixture in a greased 12-inch round pan. Flour your hands with rice flour and pat the dough until it is evenly spread in the pan. Make sure the edges are thicker and slightly go up the sides of the pan. Let the dough rise for at least 30 minutes, or until doubled in size. Optional: prior to baking the crust, sprinkle the edges with dried garlic flakes for extra flavor.

4. Bake for 10 minutes. Take out of the oven, top to your liking, and bake for an additional 25 minutes, or until the edges are golden brown.

Serves 6–8

Lamb Patties

1   LB LAMB, GROUND
½   TEASPOON GARLIC, MINCED
4   STRIPS RAW BACON
      SALT AND PEPPER TO TASTE

1. Combine lamb with garlic and seasoning. Mix well.

2. Form the lamb into four patties. Wrap each patty with a strip of bacon, using toothpicks to secure the bacon to the patties.

3. Grill, broil, or pan fry the patties until completely cooked.

4. Serve with or without a bun.

Serves 4

Mustard Glazed Salmon

½ CUP BROWN SUGAR
2 TABLESPOONS OLIVE OIL
3 TABLESPOONS HONEY
2 TABLESPOONS DIJON MUSTARD
½ SALMON, FILLETED, OR 4–6 SALMON
   STEAKS
   SALT AND LEMON PEPPER

1. Wash and dry the salmon, and sprinkle with salt and lemon pepper.

2. Whisk together the remaining ingredients.

3. Place the salmon, skin side down, on a hot grill and brush on the glaze while grilling. If using salmon steaks, roll the small ends in toward the middle and use tooth picks to secure, creating a salmon "burger"; these will grill more evenly.

4. Serve salmon medium rare.

Serves 4–6

Pizza Crust

1 TABLESPOON DRY YEAST
1/3 CUP WHITE RICE FLOUR
1/3 CUP SORGHUM FLOUR
1/2 CUP TAPIOCA STARCH
2 TABLESPOONS SWEET RICE FLOUR
2 TEASPOONS GUAR GUM
1 TEASPOON UNFLAVORED GELATIN
1 TEASPOON DRIED OREGANO FLAKES
1/2 TEASPOON SALT
1 CUP WARM WATER
1/2 TEASPOON SUGAR
1 TEASPOON OIL
1 TEASPOON VINEGAR

1. Preheat oven to 425°F.

2. Combine all of the above ingredients and beat together with an electric mixer until combined. Add more water if needed, one tablespoon at a time.

3. Place the dough on a greased 12-inch round pan. Flour your hands with rice flour and pat the dough until it is evenly spread in the pan. Make sure the edges are thicker and slightly rolled up the sides of the pan.

4. Bake for 10 minutes. Take the crust out of the oven. Top to your liking and bake for an additional 25 minutes, or until the edges are golden brown.

Serves 6–8

Salmon with Minty Mustard

2   LBS FRESH ALASKAN SALMON
1   TABLESPOON FRESH MINT,
    CRUSHED
½   TEASPOON FRESH GINGER, GRATED
2   TABLESPOONS DIJON MUSTARD
1   TABLESPOON LEMON JUICE
    SALT AND PEPPER TO TASTE

1. Preheat oven to 350°F.

2. Mix the mint, ginger, mustard, and lemon juice. Marinate the salmon in the mixture for about an hour.

3. Place the salmon in a greased baking dish and glaze with leftover marinade, sprinkling with salt and pepper to taste.

4. Bake for about 20 minutes, or until salmon is medium rare.

5. Serve with any leftover glaze.

Serves 4–6

Seafood Loaf

16–18 OZ OF CANNED SEAFOOD:
SALMON, TUNA, CRAB, OR
CHOPPED SHRIMP

1 EGG

2 TABLESPOONS LEMON JUICE

¼ CUP WHITE WINE

1 TEASPOON LEMON PEPPER

1 TEASPOON FRESH DILL,
CHOPPED FINE

1 TABLESPOON FRESH PARSLEY,
CHOPPED FINE

¼ CUP RED ONION, CHOPPED FINE

¼ CUP GLUTEN-FREE BREAD
CRUMBS

½ TEASPOON SALT

¼ TEASPOON PAPRIKA

1. Preheat oven to 350°F.

2. Prepare a regular loaf pan by spraying it with non-stick spray.

3. Blend ingredients together in a bowl. Pack ingredients into the loaf pan and bake for 20 to 30 minutes.

4. Top the seafood loaf with mushroom soup, mayonnaise, or serve plain.

Serves 4

Shepherd's Pie

2 CUPS MASHED POTATOES
½ CUP ASSORTED VEGETABLES,
FRESH OR FROZEN
1 CLOVE GARLIC, MINCED
1 TABLESPOON OLIVE OIL
¼ CUP ONION, DICED, OR 1 SCALLION,
DICED
2 CUPS COOKED MEAT (LEFTOVERS
WORK GREAT): HAM, BEEF, LAMB,
SAUSAGE
GLUTEN-FREE BREAD CRUMBS
SALT AND PEPPER TO TASTE

1. Preheat oven to 375°F.

2. Spray an 8 x 8 x 2 pan with non-stick spray. Sprinkle bread crumbs and coat the pan.

3. Heat oil and fry garlic and onion, then add meat and heat through.

4. Place meat mixture in the bottom of the pan, add veggies on top, and top with mashed potatoes. Sprinkle more bread crumbs on top.

5. Bake 30 minutes or until hot.

Serves 4

Steak with Mushrooms

4   8-OZ SIRLOIN STEAKS
    SALT AND PEPPER

Marinade
¼   CUP BALSAMIC VINEGAR
2   TABLESPOONS MOLASSES
1   CLOVE GARLIC, MINCED
1   TABLESPOON TOMATO PASTE

Topping
2   CUPS MUSHROOMS (PORTOBELLO,
    WHITE, OR OYSTER), CHOPPED
¼   CUP ONION, CHOPPED
1   CLOVE GARLIC, MINCED
2   TABLESPOONS OLIVE OIL

1. Whisk marinade together.

2. Salt and pepper the steaks, then marinate them for about 30 minutes.

3. Grill the steaks until done to your preference (20 minutes for medium).

4. Heat oil in a pan and sweat onion and garlic. Add mushrooms and fry until the mushrooms give off their juices.

5. Top the steak with mushroom mixture and serve.

Serves 4

Stuffed Peppers Bosnian Style

1   LB TURKEY, GROUND
½   CUP UNCOOKED WHITE RICE, OR
     PARTIALLY COOKED BROWN RICE
1   LARGE ONION, FINELY CHOPPED
2   CLOVES GARLIC, MINCED
1   SMALL CARROT, GRATED
1 ½ TEASPOONS VEGETABLE SOUP
     BASE POWDER
1   TEASPOON FRESH DILL WEED,
     CHOPPED
4   TABLESPOONS FRESH PARSLEY,
     CHOPPED
8   MEDIUM HUNGARIAN/GYPSY
     PEPPERS
1   MEDIUM TOMATO
     SALT AND PEPPER TO TASTE

1. Preheat oven to 425°F.

2. In a food processor combine the onion and garlic and pulse until chopped to your liking. Fry in a pan until onions become translucent. Add ground turkey and fry until completely brown. Remove from the stove and add chopped carrot, rice, vegetable soup powder, dill weed, parsley, salt and pepper.

3. Wash and core the peppers. Using a fork, pierce each pepper a couple of times to let the steam escape during baking.

4. Slice the tomato into eight disks. Stuff each pepper with the filling then use a tomato slice to close the opening to the pepper. Use remaining tomato slices for garnish and for covering the bottom of the baking pan.

5. Sprinkle peppers with a little oil and place in the oven. Bake for 40 minutes, until skin is blackened.

Serves 8

Note: For a more rustic feel, take 3 medium tomatoes, slice into wedges, and spread on the bottom of the baking pan.

Sweet Ham Bake

4–6 SLICES OF HAM

2 13-OZ CANS OF SWEET POTATOES OR YAMS, OR 2 MEDIUM COOKED SWEET POTATOES OR YAMS

½ CUP DRIED FRUIT (RAISINS, MANGOS, PINEAPPLE, PAPAYA, CRANBERRIES, ETC.)

½ CUP BROWN SUGAR

1 TEASPOON GROUND CINNAMON

¼ TEASPOON CLOVE

¼ TEASPOON NUTMEG

¼ TEASPOON FRESHLY GROUND GINGER

1. Preheat oven to 350°F.

2. Cube the ham and slice the sweet potatoes into 1-inch cubes.

3. Mix all ingredients in a 2-quart baking pan.

4. Bake for 30 minutes.

Serves 4–6

Vegetarian Stuffed Peppers

6–8 MEDIUM POTATOES, GRATED
1 LARGE ONION, FINELY CHOPPED
2 CLOVES GARLIC, MINCED
1 SMALL CARROT, GRATED
4 TABLESPOONS FRESH PARSLEY, CHOPPED
8 MEDIUM HUNGARIAN/GYPSY PEPPERS
SALT AND PEPPER TO TASTE

1. Preheat oven to 300°F.

2. Grate the potatoes and carrots. Add finely chopped onions, garlic, and parsley, seasoning to taste. Wash and core the peppers. Using a fork, pierce each pepper a couple of times to let the steam escape during baking.

3. Stuff each pepper with the filling. If you have remaining filling, use it to layer on the bottom of the baking pan. Sprinkle the peppers with a little oil prior to baking.

4. Bake for 60 minutes, until skin is light brown.

Makes 6–8 peppers

CHAPTER TEN

Pastries and Desserts

158	Almond Candies
161	Apple, Banana, and Flax Muffins
162	Apple Pear Quinoa Crisp
165	Banana Muffins
166	Caramel Sauce
169	Carrot Cake
170	Choco Crinkle Cookies
173	Chocolate Cake
174	Chocolate Chip Cookies
177	Chocolate Covered Carob Brownie
178	Chocolate Mousse
181	Coconut Crème Brûlée
182	Fig Bars
185	Forgotten Cookies
186	Frozen Fruit Drink
189	Fruit Compote Crepes
190	Fudge Brownies
193	Gingersnap Raspberry Sandwiches
194	Grand Marnier Cranberry Muffins
197	Icing
198	Orange Rosemary Pound Cake
201	Pancakes
202	Pavlina's London Bricks
205	Peach Cream Pie
206	Pie Crust
209	Raspberry Butter Cookie Sandwich
210	Rhubarb Crisp
213	Rice Pudding
214	Rum Balls
217	Scones
218	Scottish Shortbread
221	Strawberry Ambrosia
222	Tapioca Pudding
225	Tart Custard
226	Tart Crust
229	Truffles
230	Yellow Cake
233	Zucchini Bread

The Food Allergy Cookbook

Almond Candies

2 CUPS CONFECTIONERS' SUGAR

2 ½ CUPS UNSWEETENED, FINELY SHREDDED COCONUT FLAKES

¾ CUP COLD MASHED POTATOES (WITHOUT ADDED MILK OR BUTTER)

1 ½ TEASPOONS ALMOND EXTRACT (ALMOND PASTE CAN BE USED AS A SUBSTITUTE)

½ TEASPOON SALT

20 OZ FISHER CHEF'S NATURALS CHOCOLATE-FLAVORED ALMOND BARK (CONTAINS SOY LECITHIN)

PALM SEED SHORTENING, AS NEEDED

1. In a large bowl, combine first five ingredients. Line a 9-inch square pan with foil. Grease the foil then spread the coconut mixture into the pan. Use your hands to press it into the pan. Cover and chill overnight. Cut into 1 x 2 inch rectangles, cover, and freeze.

2. Over a low heat, melt the almond bark in batches and keep adding the shortening until it is thin enough for dipping and coating. You want to make sure the mixture does not boil, otherwise the bark will curdle.

3. In the meantime, line a cutting board or cookie rack with parchment paper. Take out the coconut mixture from the freezer and start dipping the pieces into the chocolate. Using a fork, take coated pieces and place them on the parchment paper.

4. Store in an airtight container.

Makes about 1 dozen

Apple, Banana, and Flax Muffins

½ CUP SUGAR
½ CUP BROWN SUGAR
½ CUP COTTONSEED SHORTENING
1 EGG
1 TEASPOON VANILLA
½ CUP MASHED BANANAS (ABOUT 2 BANANAS)
½ CUP APPLE SAUCE
2 TABLESPOONS MILK SUBSTITUTE
1 ½ TEASPOONS BAKING SODA
1 ½ CUPS FLOUR MIXTURE (SEE P.10)
1 TEASPOON GROUND CINNAMON
1 ½ TEASPOONS XANTHAN GUM
1 SOUR APPLE (GRANNY SMITH WORKS GREAT), DICED
¼ CUP FLAX SEED

1. Preheat oven to 350°F.

2. Blend sugars and shortening together with an electric hand mixer.

3. Add egg, vanilla, bananas, and milk. Slowly add dry ingredients.

4. With a spoon or rubber scraper, fold in the apple pieces and flax seed. Fill muffin pans about ¾ full. You can use either greased muffin pans or paper muffin cups.

5. Bake for 25 to 30 minutes.

Makes about 1 dozen

Apple Pear Quinoa Crisp

CRUST
1 ½ CUPS QUINOA FLAKES
¼ CUP BROWN SUGAR
4 TABLESPOONS MARGARINE,
MELTED
2 TABLESPOONS FLOUR MIXTURE
(SEE P.10)
½ TEASPOON CINNAMON, GROUND
¼ TEASPOON SALT

FILLING
3 PEARS, SLICED THIN, ACIDULATED
3 GRANNY SMITH APPLES, SLICED
THIN, ACIDULATED
CARAMEL SAUCE (OPTIONAL)

1. Preheat oven to 350°F.

2. Mix the crust mixture and pack about ¾ of it firmly into a 9 x 13 x 2 inch pan.

3. Alternate the layers of apple and pear slices. If using caramel sauce, drizzle over top of the fruit. Cover the pie with the reserved crumble/crust.

4. Bake for about 45 minutes. Let cool before cutting and serving.

5. Serve with additional caramel sauce or with Rice Dream ice cream.

Serves 6–8

Banana Muffins

½ CUP SUGAR
½ CUP BROWN SUGAR
½ CUP COTTONSEED SHORTENING
1 EGG
1 TEASPOON VANILLA
1 CUP MASHED BANANAS (ABOUT 2)
2 TABLESPOONS MILK SUBSTITUTE
1 ½ TEASPOONS BAKING SODA
1 ½ CUPS FLOUR MIXTURE (SEE P.10)
1 TEASPOON GROUND CINNAMON
1 ½ TEASPOONS XANTHAN GUM

1. Preheat oven to 350°F.

2. Blend the sugars and shortening together using an electric hand mixer.

3. Add egg, vanilla, bananas, and milk. Slowly add dry ingredients.

4. Fill muffin cups about ¾ full. You can use either paper muffin cups or greased muffin tins.

5. Bake for 25 to 30 minutes.

Makes about 1 dozen

Caramel Sauce

1 CUP SUGAR
2 TABLESPOONS AGAVE NECTAR
¼ CUP WATER
¼ CUP COCONUT MILK
1 TABLESPOON MARGARINE
PINCH OF SALT

1. Combine sugar, agave nectar, and water in a sauce pan. Heat to boiling and then reduce to low. Monitor and stir or swirl the pan to distribute heat evenly and to dissolve the sugar. Let the mixture heat until it is a deep amber color (be very careful as it is extremely hot!).

2. Remove from heat and carefully add salt, margarine, and coconut milk (mixture will boil up). Let mixture cool.

3. Use as a topping for ice dream, to garnish on apple pear crisp, or for your own ideas!

Makes about 1 cup

Carrot Cake

CAKE

1 ½ CUPS FLOUR MIXTURE (SEE P.10)
(OPTIONAL: SUBSTITUTE ½ CUP
ALMOND FLOUR FOR ½ CUP

FLOUR MIXTURE)

¼ CUP WHITE SUGAR
¾ CUP BROWN SUGAR
¾ TEASPOON BAKING SODA
¾ TEASPOON BAKING POWDER
2 CUPS SHREDDED CARROTS
3 EGGS
¼ CUP OIL
½ CUP UNSWEETENED APPLESAUCE
1 TEASPOON GROUND CINNAMON
½ TEASPOON FRESHLY GROUND
GINGER
½ CUP RAISINS
1 TEASPOON VANILLA

ICING

1 TEASPOON VANILLA
3 CUPS POWDERED SUGAR
½ CUP CREAM CHEESE (SOY OR COW)

1. Preheat oven to 350°F.

2. Cream the sugar, eggs, applesauce, and oil. Add shredded carrots and raisins. Slowly blend in flours, spices, baking powder, and baking soda.

3. Pour into muffin cups (with paper cups) or into a cake pan.

4. Bake 25–30 minutes. Cool.

5. For icing, whip cream cheese and vanilla. Slowly incorporate powdered sugar. Refrigerate for 1 hour.

6. Ice the completely cooled cake.

Serves 8–12

Choco Crinkle Cookies

3   EGGS
1 ½   CUPS SUGAR
4   OZ UNSWEETENED CHOCOLATE
     OR ½ CUP BAKER'S COCOA
     POWDER AND ¼ CUP OIL
½   CUP VEGETABLE OIL
2   TEASPOONS BAKING POWDER
2   TEASPOONS VANILLA
1 ¼ TO 1 ½   CUPS FLOUR MIXTURE (SEE
     P.10)
½   CUP POWDERED SUGAR
1   TABLESPOON GROUND CINNAMON

1. Preheat oven to 375°F.

2. Blend together eggs, sugar, chocolate, oil, baking powder, and vanilla. Slowly add flour until dough is stiff and hard to stir. Refrigerate for 1–2 hours.

3. Using a zip-top bag, combine powdered sugar with cinnamon. Portion out the cinnamon/sugar mix in a shallow plate. Roll dough into 1-inch balls and roll balls in powdered cinnamon/sugar mix. Place on baking pan 2 inches apart and bake for 8–10 minutes.

4. As soon as the cookies are removed from the oven take the flat bottom of a glass and carefully squish the cookies flat. Let cool and serve.

Makes about 2 dozen cookies

Chocolate Cake

2 CUPS FLOUR MIXTURE (SEE P.10)
1 TEASPOON XANTHAN GUM
1 TEASPOON BAKING SODA
½ TEASPOON SALT
¾ CUP SUGAR
⅓ CUP COCOA POWDER
½ CUP CANOLA OIL
1 TEASPOON VINEGAR OR LEMON
   JUICE
1 TEASPOON VANILLA
½ CUP MASHED BANANAS OR
   APPLESAUCE
1 CUP WATER

1. Preheat oven to 350°F.

2. Mix the dry ingredients in a bowl. In a second bowl, mix the wet ingredients. In a third bowl, combine the wet and dry ingredients, alternating dry and wet.

3. Pour the mixture into a 9 x 9 greased pan. Bake for about 35 minutes.

4. Either ice the cake with a simple powdered sugar icing or dust with powdered sugar.

Serves 4–6

Chocolate Chip Cookies

½ CUP COTTONSEED SHORTENING
½ CUP MARGARINE
½ CUP SUGAR
1 CUP BROWN SUGAR
½ TEASPOON BAKING SODA
2 EGGS
1 TEASPOON VANILLA
2 ⅓ CUPS FLOUR MIXTURE (SEE P.10)
2 ½ TEASPOONS XANTHAN GUM
12 OZ. ENJOY LIFE SEMI-SWEET
CHOCOLATE CHIPS

1. Preheat oven to 375° F.

2. Cream the margarine and shortening with the sugars. Blend until very smooth.

3. Add baking soda, eggs, and vanilla. Blend in flour and xanthan gum. Add chocolate chips.

4. Spoon batter onto a parchment-lined baking pan, spacing cookies about 1 inch apart. Cookies should be about golf ball sized.

5. Bake 8–10 minutes. Cool on wire rack.

Makes about 2 ½ dozen

Hot Tip:

To keep your brown sugar soft, try placing a slice of apple with the brown sugar and seal in a plastic container.

Chocolate Covered Carob Brownie

BROWNIE

2 ½   CUPS MILK SUBSTITUTE
1 ¼   CUPS VEGETABLE OIL
½   CUP SUGAR
1   CUP FLOUR MIXTURE (SEE P.10)
¾   CUP CAROB FLOUR
2   TEASPOONS BAKING POWDER

TOPPING

  7-OZ DARK CHOCOLATE BAR
4   TABLESPOONS MILK SUBSTITUTE
4   TABLESPOONS SUGAR
1   TABLESPOON MARGARINE

1. Preheat oven to 350°F.

2. In a bowl, combine all wet ingredients. In another bowl combine all the dry ingredients. Slowly add the wet ingredients to the dry. Use a hand whisk to get an even consistency.

3. Transfer the mixture to a greased 9 x 13 pan and bake for 30 minutes, or until a toothpick inserted in the middle comes out clean.

4. While the brownies are baking, combine the ingredients for the topping. Place the bowl on the stove while the brownies are baking. In 30 minutes all the ingredients will melt, without any additional effort. Using a whisk, stir the chocolate mix to combine.

5. Pour the mixture over the hot brownies and serve.

Makes one dozen brownies

Chocolate Mousse

1 TABLESPOON UNSALTED
  MARGARINE (COTTON SEED,
  SAFFLOWER, OR SOY)
½ TEASPOON BUTTER FLAVORING
  6 OZ SEMI-SWEET DARK CHOCOLATE
  (DAIRY FREE)
2 CUPS POWDERED SUGAR
½ TABLESPOON FLAVORING (RUM,
  GRAND MARNIER, ETC)
  8 OZ PACKAGE NON-DAIRY
  WHIPPING CREAM

1. Leave margarine at room temperature for a couple of hours to soften.

2. Melt the chocolate using a double boiler method or the microwave. Let it cool before adding to the margarine.

3. In a bowl, cream the margarine and flavorings. Add melted chocolate and powdered sugar. Place in a refrigerator for a few minutes while you follow the directions for the non-dairy whipping cream. Once you have made the whipped cream add it to the butter mixture and mix long enough to evenly combine the two.

4. Chill and serve.

Serves 4

*TO MAKE A RASPBERRY CHOCOLATE MOUSSE, ADD ¼ CUP UNSWEETENED
  RASPBERRY JAM WHEN CREAMING THE BUTTER.
*TO MAKE AN ORANGE CHOCOLATE MOUSSE, ADD RIND OF 2 ORANGES
  WHILE CREAMING THE BUTTER.

Coconut Crème Brûlée

1 ¼ CUPS COCONUT MILK
¾ CUP MILK SUBSTITUTE
¼ CUP SUGAR
1 VANILLA BEAN
6 EGG YOLKS, BEATEN WELL
¼ CUP SUGAR

1. Preheat oven to 350°F.

2. Whisk together the coconut milk, milk substitute, eggs, and sugar in a medium sauce pan. Add the vanilla bean (cut lengthwise and scrape out the seeds, adding them to the mixture along with the bean) and heat over medium heat, whisking often for about 20 minutes or until just boiling.

3. Strain the final sauce, being sure to get out the bits of the vanilla beans (though seeds should remain, speckling the mixture).

4. Pour the crème sauce evenly into four ramekins. Place ramekins in one pan (large enough to hold all four). Slowly add boiling water (ban Marie) to the pan and bake for 45 minutes or until crème jiggles.

5. Refrigerate for 6–8 hours (best if left overnight).

6. Pull out Crème Brûlée 30 minutes to 1 hour before serving and wait until it reaches room temperature. Sprinkle sugar on each ramekin (1 tablespoon each), making sure that the sugar coats the Crème Brûlée.

7. Using a small kitchen torch or boiler burn the sugar until crisp and golden. Serve immediately.

Makes 4 servings

Fig Bars

FIG FILLING

3   CUPS DRIED FIGS (ABOUT 1 LB),
    ROUGHLY CHOPPED
¼   CUP HONEY OR SUGAR SYRUP
1   CUP RED WINE
1   CUP WATER
¼   TEASPOON CINNAMON
½   TEASPOON FINELY GROUND PEPPER

PASTRY DOUGH

½   LB (2 STICKS) UNSALTED,
    COTTONSEED MARGARINE
½   TEASPOON BUTTER FLAVOR
½   CUP SUGAR
1   LARGE EGG
2   EGG YOLKS
1   TEASPOON PURE VANILLA EXTRACT
    ZEST OF ONE LEMON
    PINCH OF SALT
3   CUPS FLOUR MIXTURE (SEE P.10)
1   EGG YOLK PLUS
1   TEASPOON MILK FOR EGG WASH

1. Preheat oven to 375°F.

2. Remove stems from the figs. Halve them then pulse them a few times in a food processor until coarsely chopped.

3. Combine the remaining filling ingredients in a nonstick frying pan and cook over low heat, stirring often, until liquid is reduced. It will take approximately 10 to 15 minutes.

4. Leave filling to cool. It can be stored in the refrigerator up to 1 week. Bring to room temperature before using.

5. To make pastry dough, combine margarine, butter flavor, and sugar. Using an electric mixer beat on a medium speed until margarine is light and fluffy. Add one whole egg and an egg yolk, vanilla, and zest; mix well. Add flour and salt. Mix on low just until dough comes together.

6. Divide the dough in half; wrap each half in a plastic

wrap. Chill until firm, about 1 hour.

7. Dust a large piece of parchment paper with flour and roll out half of the dough to a rectangle approximately 9 x 14 in size. Using a rolling pin, transfer this rectangle into a baking pan. Spread filling evenly over the pastry. Roll remaining dough and use it to cover the filling. Chill for an hour.

8. In a small bowl beat together the remaining egg yolk and the milk, and set aside. Score the dough into 1 ¼ x 3 inch bars. Lightly brush with egg wash. Bake until golden brown, 25–30 minutes.

9. Transfer to a wire rack until cool. Cut into bars.

Yields 24 bars

Forgotten Cookies

2 EGG WHITES
⅛ TEASPOON CREAM OF TARTAR
¾ CUP SUGAR
1 CUP ENJOY LIFE SEMI-SWEET
   CHOCOLATE CHIPS OR CAROB CHIPS
½ TEASPOON VANILLA
½ TEASPOON PEPPERMINT EXTRACT

1. Preheat oven to 350°F.

2. In a metal bowl, beat egg whites and cream of tartar until hard peaks form. Slowly add sugar and extracts. Carefully fold in chips.

3. Drop by the teaspoon on greased cookie sheet. Place in the oven and turn off the heat.

4. Leave overnight and forget about the cookies. The meringue will harden overnight.

5. Store in an airtight container.

Makes about 2 ½ dozen

Frozen Fruit Drink

½   CUP FROZEN FRUIT JUICE
½   CUP SUGAR
½   CUP VANILLA ICE CREAM (SOY, RICE, MILK)
12   ICE CUBES
1   TEASPOON VANILLA
¼–½ CUP MILK SUBSTITUTE

1. Place all ingredients in a blender. Blend until mixture is relatively smooth.

2. Serve in chilled glasses with a straw.

Serves 2–4

Fruit Compote Crepes

2   DOZEN DESSERT CREPES
1   CUP APPLES, CHOPPED
1   CUP PEACHES OR NECTARINES, CHOPPED
1   CUP BERRIES (BLUEBERRIES, CUT STRAWBERRIES, RASPBERRIES, ETC.)
1   CUP SUGAR
½   TEASPOON GROUND CINNAMON
    PINCH OF PEPPER
½   CUP ORANGE JUICE

1. Combine all ingredients in a large sauce pan.

2. Bring to a boil and simmer for 20 minutes.

3. Spoon into dessert crepes and serve hot. They are great topped with Rice Dream ice cream.

Serves 4–6

Fudge Brownies

½ CUP MARGARINE

2 OZ UNSWEETENED COCOA (OR 6 TABLESPOONS COCOA POWDER)

1 TEASPOON INSTANT COFFEE

2 EGGS

1 CUP SUGAR

2 TEASPOONS VANILLA EXTRACT (ADD ALMOND EXTRACT FOR AMARETTO FLAVORED BROWNIES AS AN ALTERNATIVE)

¾ CUP FLOUR MIXTURE (SEE P.10)

½ CUP ENJOY LIFE SEMI-SWEET CHOCOLATE CHIPS OR CAROB CHIPS

1. Preheat oven to 350°F.

2. Prepare an 8 x 8 pan and spray with non-stick spray.

3. Melt margarine in a saucepan. Add cocoa and coffee and mix. Stir in eggs, sugar, and vanilla extract. Blend until smooth. Slowly incorporate flour. Finally add chocolate chips.

4. Place mixture in the prepared pan and bake for 20–30 minutes, or until a toothpick inserted in the middle comes out clean.

5. Cool and serve.

Makes 9 brownies

Hot Tip:

Many of the spray oils (like Pam) contain wheat as a propellant. In most higher-end kitchen stores you can find oil atomizers. Use this with canola oil for the same effect.

Gingersnap Raspberry Sandwiches

1 STICK (¼ LB) UNSALTED
  COTTONSEED MARGARINE, ROOM
  TEMPERATURE
¼ CUP COTTONSEED SHORTENING
2 CUPS SUGAR, DIVIDED
3 CUPS FLOUR MIXTURE (SEE P.10)
2 TEASPOONS BAKING SODA
1 TEASPOON CINNAMON, GROUND
1 TEASPOON GINGER, GROUND
⅛ CUP MOLASSES
1 LARGE EGG, BEATEN
1 CUP LOW-SUGAR RASPBERRY JAM

1. Preheat oven to 375°F.

2. In a bowl combine margarine, shortening, and 1 cup sugar. Using an electric mixer, cream the shortening until it's light and fluffy.

3. In a separate bowl, sift together flour, baking soda, cinnamon, and ginger. Add egg and molasses to the butter mixture and beat until combined. Reduce speed to low and slowly add dry ingredients until well blended.

4. Divide dough into 24 balls. Roll each ball in the remaining 1 cup of sugar then transfer to a prepared baking sheet, spacing balls 3 inches apart.

5. Bake until the cookie is flattened and the surface is cracked, about 10 minutes.

6. Transfer cookies to a wire rack to cool. Once cookies have completely cooled, spread about 2 teaspoons of jam on half of the cookies. Place a second cookie on the top to make a sandwich.

Makes 24 cookies

NOTE: IF THE COOKIES ARE TOO HARD, PLACE THEM INTO A CLOSED CONTAINER FOR AN HOUR. THEY WILL ABSORB THE MOISTURE FROM THE FILLING. HOWEVER, DO NOT LEAVE THEM IN A CLOSED CONTAINER, BECAUSE IF THEY ABSORB TOO MUCH MOISTURE THEY WILL BECOME MUSHY.

Grand Marnier Cranberry Muffins

½ CUP + ⅛ CUP ORANGE JUICE
⅛ CUP GRAND MARNIER LIQUOR
⅓ CUP VEGETABLE OIL
1 CUP DRIED CRANBERRIES, CHOPPED
1 ½ CUPS FLOUR MIXTURE (SEE P.10)
¼ CUP SORGHUM FLOUR
¾ CUP SUGAR
1 TEASPOON BAKING SODA
1 TEASPOON CREAM OF TARTAR
¼ TEASPOON SALT
1 TEASPOON ORANGE ZEST
2 EGG WHITES

1. Preheat oven to 400°F.

2. Combine orange juice, the Grand Marnier, and oil; set aside.

3. In a large bowl combine the flours, sugar, salt, baking soda, cream of tartar, and orange zest. In another bowl beat the egg whites until frothy. Combine the rest of the liquids with the egg whites.

4. Add the egg mixture and cranberries to the flour, stirring until just moist.

5. Using ¼ cup measure, divide the batter among 12 muffin cups fitted with paper liners.

6. Bake for 25 minutes or until a toothpick inserted in the middle comes out clean.

Makes 1 dozen

Icing

2   TABLESPOONS SAFFLOWER
    MARGARINE, SOFTENED
3   TABLESPOONS MILK SUBSTITUTE
1   34-OZ BAG POWDERED SUGAR
    (NOTE: THIS MAY CONTAIN CORN
    STARCH)
1   TABLESPOON VANILLA

1. With an electric mixer, blend margarine, vanilla, and milk, slowly adding powdered sugar. Blend until completely mixed. Depending on humidity, you may need more milk substitute. Mix to desired consistency.

2. Use as a glaze (if thin and liquid-like), or an icing (if firm).

Makes 2 cups of icing

*TRY EXPERIMENTING BY ADDING DIFFERENT FLAVORING FOR DIFFERENT TASTES. LEMON, ORANGE, AND PEPPERMINT ARE ALL WONDERFUL FLAVORS.

Orange Rosemary Pound Cake

JUICE AND ZEST OF 1 ORANGE
(ADD EXTRA ORANGE JUICE TO
EQUAL ½ CUP IF NECESSARY)
1   LARGE SPRIG FRESH ROSEMARY,
CRUSHED
1   TABLESPOON TAPIOCA STARCH
½   CUP MARGARINE
3   EGGS
1 ½   CUPS FLOUR MIXTURE (SEE P.10)
¼   TEASPOON BAKING POWDER
1   CUP SUGAR
1   TEASPOON VANILLA
1   TEASPOON BUTTER FLAVORING

1. Preheat oven to 350°F.

2. Spray a loaf pan with
cooking spray.

3. Make a slurry out of
tapioca starch and orange
juice. Heat slurry and
crushed rosemary in a
small sauce pan and until
thick, stirring often.

4. Cream the margarine and sugar. Add eggs, vanilla,
butter flavor, and baking powder. Mix until smooth
and slightly lightened in color. Slowly add flour, ½ cup
at a time.

5. Place mixture in the loaf pan and bake for
approximately 75 minutes, or until a toothpick comes
out clean when inserted in the middle.

Makes 1 loaf

Hot Tip:

Wedding cakes are notorious for being filled with
wheat and dairy. Try using the Orange Rosemary
Poundcake recipe instead. Try baking the batter in a
cupcake pan. Then, place the cupcakes on a dessert
tier. Decorate around the cakes with edible flowers.
Your guests will love having their own "wedding
cakes" to themselves—and you'll enjoy partaking in
the dessert!

Pancakes

1 CUP SORGHUM FLOUR
1 TABLESPOON SUGAR
2 TEASPOONS BAKING POWDER
¼ TEASPOON SALT
1 EGG
1 CUP MILK SUBSTITUTE
2 TABLESPOONS OIL
½ CUP FRUIT (BERRIES, APPLES, BANANAS, ETC.), NUTS, CHOCOLATE CHIPS, ETC., FOR ADDED FLAVOR

1. Mix all ingredients in a blender.

2. Pour about ¼ cup of batter into large hot frying pan or griddle. Turn over when nicely browned.

3. Serve with maple syrup.

Makes about 1 dozen

Hot Tip:

If you tend to be a "run out the door without breakfast" type, try making an extra batch of pancakes. You can freeze them or keep them in the fridge and heat in the microwave when you need a quick meal. They travel very well and are a nutritious "breakfast on the go"!

Pavlina's London Bricks

DOUGH

3 EGG YOLKS + 1 WHOLE EGG, ROOM TEMPERATURE
1 ½ CUPS FLOUR MIXTURE (SEE P.10)
¼ CUP WALNUTS, GROUND (USE CHEESE GRATER), OR ¼ CUP FLAXSEED MEAL
½ TEASPOON XANTHAN GUM
1 TEASPOON BAKING POWDER
1 TABLESPOON GRATED CITRUS ZEST (LEMON, LIME, OR ORANGE)
½ CUP PALM SHORTENING
3 TEASPOONS WATER
¼ TEASPOON BUTTER FLAVOR
½ CUP GRANULATED SUGAR

FILLING

½ CUP SMACKER'S LOW-SUGAR APRICOT JAM

TOPPING

3 EGG WHITES
¼ TEASPOON RICE VINEGAR OR ⅓ TEASPOON CREAM OF TARTAR
1 CUP GRANULATED SUGAR
1 CUP GROUND WALNUTS OR 1 CUP FLAXSEED MEAL

1. Preheat oven to 350°F.

2. Separate the eggs and set aside all egg whites in a medium metal bowl.

3. In a bowl or zip-lock bag combine all of the dry ingredients.

4. In a separate bowl beat the shortening, granulated sugar, one whole egg, and the egg yolks. Add up to ½ of the dry ingredients. Beat on medium speed until thoroughly combined. Stir in the remaining dry ingredients and knead using your fingers. It will make soft and sticky dough.

5. Transfer the dough to a greased 9 x 9 in square pan and pat it using your hands.

6. Bake for 15 minutes.

7. Meanwhile, add the vinegar/cream of tartar to the egg whites and, using clean beaters and a metal bowl, beat on the highest speed until soft peaks form. Gradually add the sugar. Fold in the walnuts/flax meal to create meringue.

8. Take the dough out of the oven and spread the apricot jam over it. Top with meringue. Return to the oven and bake for about 20 minutes longer, or until the top is golden brown. The crust will rise and crack up.

9. Once you take it out of the oven it will deflate and become very crisp. Cool. Cut in small wedges.

Serves 12

Peach Cream Pie

1 PIE CRUST, PRE-BAKED (SEE P.207)
6–8 FRESH PEACHES, PEELED
AND HALVED, OR 2 ½ OZ CAN OF
PEACHES, DRAINED
¾ CUP SUGAR
4 TABLESPOONS RICE FLOUR
1 ½ TEASPOONS GROUND CINNAMON
¾ CUP COCONUT MILK

1. Preheat oven to 425°F.

2. Mix sugar, flour, and cinnamon. Pour about ¼ cinnamon mixture into the base of the pie shell. Place peaches, dome side up, in the pie shell. Fill in spaces with cuts of peaches (don't forget to place a cut under each dome of peach). Sprinkle the remaining cinnamon mixture over peaches, ensuring that there is good even coverage. Slowly pour coconut milk over the peaches, lifting them and allowing the coconut milk to drain under the peach domes and fill entire pie. There may be some coconut milk left over.

3. Place pie on a foil-lined baking sheet and bake in the oven for about 35–45 minutes.

4. The pie is done when cream appears mostly solid (a bit of a jiggle when shaken).

5. Cool and serve with Rice Dream ice cream.

Serves 6–8

Pie Crust

1 CRUST

1 CUP TAPIOCA STARCH
¼ CUP POTATO STARCH
¼ CUP GLUTINOUS RICE FLOUR
³⁄₈ CUP SWEET RICE FLOUR
½ TEASPOON XANTHAN GUM
¼ TEASPOON SALT
½ TEASPOON BAKING POWDER
1 ½ TABLESPOONS SUGAR

SHORTENING MIX

½ CUP COTTONSEED SHORTENING
3 TABLESPOONS COLD WATER
¼ TEASPOON BUTTER FLAVORING
2 CRUSTS
½ CUP TAPIOCA STARCH
½ CUP POTATO STARCH
½ CUP GLUTINOUS RICE FLOUR
¾ CUP SWEET RICE FLOUR
1 TEASPOON XANTHAN GUM
½ TEASPOON SALT
1 TEASPOON BAKING POWDER
3 TABLESPOONS SUGAR

SHORTENING MIX

1 CUP COTTONSEED SHORTENING
6 TABLESPOONS COLD WATER
¼ TEASPOON BUTTER FLAVORING

1. Blend the dry ingredients together then cut in shortening and butter flavor.

2. As the mix begins to crumble, add the water. Continue mixing until it resembles a loose biscuit dough.

3. Spray two long (24") pieces of wax paper with cooking spray. Scoop the dough onto one piece of greased wax paper and cover with the other piece, grease side down.

4. With your hands slowly spread the dough to the edges of the wax paper in a roughly round shape and until the dough is about ¼-inch thick.

5. Remove the top layer of wax paper. Carefully using the other piece of wax paper, move the crust into a pie pan, fluting the edges.

Raspberry Butter Cookie Sandwich

4   EGGS
1   CUP SUGAR
2   TEASPOONS VANILLA EXTRACT ZEST
    OF ONE LEMON
¾   CUP COTTONSEED SHORTENING
¼   CUP MARGARINE
1   CUP HIGH-PROTEIN FLOUR
    (GARBANZO. SORGHUM, ETC.)
3   CUPS FLOUR MIXTURE (SEE P.10)
4   TEASPOONS BAKING POWDER
    LOW-SUGAR RASPBERRY JAM
    12 OZ DARK CHOCOLATE FOR
    DIPPING

1. Preheat oven to 375°F.

2. In a bowl cream the shortening, sugar, vanilla extract, and lemon zest. Add eggs one by one and beat until mixture is light and fluffy.

3. Combine dry ingredients and sift until well combined. Set your mixer on a slow speed and gradually add the flour mix to the shortening. The dough will become smooth and soft.

4. Line 4 baking sheets with parchment paper or aluminum foil. Place a large start tip into a pastry bag and fill the bag half-full with the cookie dough. Using the pastry bag, pipe cookie dough into rosettes and onto a cooking sheet. The rosettes should be approximately 1 inch in diameter and spaced 1 ½ inches apart.

5. Place cookie sheets into a fridge for an hour, so the cookie dough can chill.

6. Bake for 12 minutes. Cookies will not brown.

7. When done, take cookies out of the oven and place on a cookie rack to cool. After they are fully cooled, place 1–2 teaspoons of low sugar raspberry jam on the bottom of one cookie and cover with another cookie. Dip half of the cookie sandwich into melted chocolate and place on parchment paper to dry.

Makes 40–44 cookies

Rhubarb Crisp

CRUST
2 CUPS FLOUR MIXTURE (SEE P.10)
1 CUP ROLLED BARLEY, SPELT,
    OR OATS
1 CUP BROWN SUGAR
¾ CUP MARGARINE (BUTTER, SOY,
    SHORTENING), MELTED
1 TEASPOON GROUND CINNAMON
1 TEASPOON BUTTER EXTRACT

FILLING
8 CUPS RHUBARB, CUT UP IN ¼–½
    INCH PIECES
2 CUPS SUGAR
3 EGGS
1 ½ TEASPOONS VANILLA

1. Preheat oven to 350°F.

2. Melt margarine and mix with other crust ingredients. Pack ¾ of the crust mixture on the bottom of a 9 x 13 inch pan. Save remainder for topping.

3. Mix the filling ingredients and pour over crust. Sprinkle remaining crust mixture over the top.

4. Bake for 40–45 minutes. Serve warm or cold.

Serves 8–10

Rice Pudding

3   EGGS
1   CUP COOKED RICE (CHINESE
    TAKEOUT WORKS GREAT!)
⅓   CUP SUGAR
½   TEASPOON SALT
1   TABLESPOON GROUND CINNAMON
1   TEASPOON NUTMEG
¾   CUP COCONUT MILK
¾   CUP MILK SUBSTITUTE
½   CUP RAISINS OR OTHER DRIED
    FRUIT
1   TEASPOON VANILLA

1. Preheat oven to 350°F.

2. Combine all ingredients and pour into a 2-quart container.

3. Bake in the oven for 45–50 minutes in a ban Marie. The pudding is done if a knife inserted into the center comes out clean.

4. Cool for a minimum of 30 minutes. Serve hot or cold.

Serves 4

Rum Balls

10 OZ PITTED DATES
6 TABLESPOONS FINELY CHOPPED, UNSWEETENED COCONUT FLAKES
¼ CUP DUTCH PROCESSED COCOA
1 CUP FINELY CHOPPED, UNSWEETENED COCONUT FLAKES, FOR ROLLING BRANDY OR RUM TO TASTE

1. Place dates, 6 tablespoons coconut flakes, and cocoa powder into food processor. Pulse on high until it forms a ball. Depending on how moist the dates are you may add water or liquor by tablespoon to help form the dough. If you have a small food processor you can do the above in 3 batches.

2. Use a 1 tablespoon measuring cup to scoop out the mix. Using your hands (disposable gloves help) form a ball, and then roll into the remaining coconut flakes until completely covered.

Makes one dozen

VARIATIONS:
- SUBSTITUTE COCONUT FLAKES WITH NUTS OF YOUR CHOICE.
- USE MARASCHINO CHERRIES AS A CENTER FOR EACH RUM BALL.

Scones

¼ CUP FAT (VEGETABLE OIL, ANY TYPE OF MARGARINE, BUTTER)

¾ CUP MILK (RICE, SOY, OAT)

1 EGG OR 1 TEASPOON FLAX SEED MEAL BOILED IN ¼ CUP WATER

1 TABLESPOON SUGAR FOR SAVORY SCONES, DOUBLE FOR SWEETER VERSION

1 CUP RICE FLOUR

¼ CUP HIGH-PROTEIN FLOUR (GARBANZO, FAVA BEAN, SORGHUM)

1 TEASPOON XANTHAN GUM/ GUAR GUM

½ TEASPOON SALT

1 ½ TEASPOONS CREAM OF TARTAR

¾ TEASPOON BAKING SODA

½ TEASPOON FLAVOR INGREDIENT (CURRANTS, GRATED CHEESE ALTERNATIVES, FINELY CHOPPED HAM, ETC.)

1. Preheat oven to 420°F.

2. Grease a nonstick baking sheet. Cover the baking sheet with aluminum foil and grease the foil (this makes it easier to clean).

3. In a bowl combine fat, egg, and milk, mixing with an electric mixer. Add all the rest of the ingredients other than the flavor ingredient. Mix with the mixer until just combined.

4. Add your flavor ingredient last and mix gently. The dough should be soft. Transfer the dough to the prepared baking sheet, patting with a spatula into 9-inch circle.

5. Bake 15–20 minutes until deeply browned. For crispier wedge-shaped pieces, cut into 8 wedges with a sharp knife before baking.

Makes 8 scones

Scottish Shortbread

1 CUP MARGARINE
2 CUPS SWEET RICE FLOUR
¼ CUP GRANULATED SUGAR
¼ CUP BROWN SUGAR, FIRMLY
 PACKED
1 TEASPOON LEMON EXTRACT

1. Preheat oven to 350°F.

2. Grease an 8-inch round pan and line the bottom with an 8-inch disk of wax paper.

3. Cream the margarine and sugars with an electric beater. Add lemon extract then slowly incorporate flour into the mix; the mix will be crumbly but will clump when pressed together. Pack the mixture into the pan with your fingers.

4. Bake 45 minutes then remove from the oven. Cut $2/3$ down into the batter forming wedges. Continue baking for another 15 minutes until lightly browned.

5. Cool in the pan for 30 minutes. Carefully invert, removing the shortbread from the pan. Cool completely.

6. Dip into bittersweet chocolate as a garnish if you like.

Serves 8–10

* THIS RECIPE CAN ALSO BE USED AS A CRUST FOR SWEET PIES,
TARTS, ETC.

Strawberry Ambrosia

PIE CRUST

1	CUP FLOUR MIXTURE (SEE P.10)
¼	CUP ALMOND FLOUR
⅓	CUP SHORTENING
4–5	TABLESPOONS COLD WATER
¼	TEASPOON SALT
1	TABLESPOON SUGAR

PIE FILLING

3–4	CUPS FRESH STRAWBERRIES, SLICED
2	CUPS POWDERED SUGAR
½	CUP TAPIOCA FLOUR
1 ½	TEASPOONS VANILLA
3	EGGS, BEATEN
½	CUP COCONUT MILK

1. Preheat oven to 350°F.

2. Prepare the pie crust by cutting shortening into flours, sugar, and salt. Add water until the dough is crumbly but holds together. Roll out between two sheets of wax paper. Place in a 9-inch pie pan.

3. Grease a 12-inch piece of foil (dull side up) and place that on the prepared dough. Add dried beans or pie beads and pre-bake for 15–20 minutes.

4. Cut up strawberries. In a large zip-lock bag, blend flour and powdered sugar, add strawberries, and mix until they are coated.

5. Beat the eggs, vanilla, and coconut milk. Pour strawberries and egg mixture into the pie shell, lifting strawberries to ensure egg mixture is even in the pie shell.

6. Bake for 40 minutes or until eggs have set.

Serves 6–8

Tapioca Pudding

3   TABLESPOONS GRANULATED
     TAPIOCA PEARLS
⅓   CUP SUGAR
½   CUP COCONUT MILK
2 ½ CUPS MILK SUBSTITUTE
2   EGGS
1   VANILLA BEAN, CUT LENGTHWISE,
     BEANS SCRAPED OUT, AND
     PLACED IN PAN

1. In a medium sauce pan, combine all ingredients. Let the mixture rest for 5 minutes.

2. Slowly heat (on medium low) until it comes to a full boil, whisking constantly. Strain out the vanilla bean.

3. Cool in the pan for 20 minutes. Serve warm or chill.

Serves 4–6

Tart Custard

4 EGG YOLKS
½ CUP SUGAR
½ CUP FLOUR MIXTURE (SEE P.10)
2 CUPS COCONUT MILK
1 CUP NON-DAIRY WHIPPING CREAM
(ADD FOR PUDDING CONSISTENCY)
1 TEASPOON VANILLA EXTRACT
1 TEASPOON EXTRACT FLAVORING OF
YOUR CHOICE (ORANGE, ALMOND,
ETC.)

1. In a large bowl, beat the egg yolks and sugar with an electric mixer on high speed until the eggs appear pale and thick. Add flavoring and continue to mix but this time on low speed until evenly combined.

2. In a double boiler bring coconut milk and non-dairy whipping cream to a simmer. Add egg mixture to the boiling milk.

3. Using a silicone spatula, stir the custard while scraping the bottom of the double boiler. Cook the custard until it is thick or reaches the consistency of pudding.

4. Remove from heat and completely cool.

Serves 6–8

*THE CUSTARD CAN BE USED AS A FILLING FOR TARTS AND PIES, OR SERVED AS A PUDDING. IF USING IT AS A TART FILLING, COMBINE IT WITH FRESH FRUIT AND APPLE JELLY. FILL THE TART CRUST WITH FILLING. ARRANGE THE FRESH FRUIT ON TOP. BRING THE APPLE JELLY TO A BOIL IN A SMALL SAUCE PAN. USING A SPOON OR PASTRY BRUSH, POUR THE APPLE JELLY OVER THE FRESH FRUIT TO KEEP IT IN PLACE.

Tart Crust

TART CRUST

1 ½	CUPS FLOUR MIXTURE (SEE P.10)
½	CUP PALM OIL SHORTENING
3	TEASPOONS COLD WATER
½	TEASPOON SALT
1	EGG
3	TABLESPOONS SUGAR
1	TEASPOON BUTTER EXTRACT

EGG WASH

1	EGG YOLK FOR EGG WASH
1	TABLESPOON WATER

FILLING OPTIONS

1	CUP TART CUSTARD OR 1 LB FRESH RASPBERRIES + ¾ CUP STRAWBERRY JELLY

1. Preheat oven to 400°F.

2. Combine dry ingredients and set aside.

3. Cream shortening, water, egg, and butter extract. Add dry ingredients to the shortening mixture and use your hands to combine. You will get soft dough.

4. If using miniature molds split into 4 parts and place in the refrigerator for 30 minutes. Dough can be simply patted into the molds using your hands. Bake for 8 minutes.

5. While the tart crust is baking, combine egg yolk and 1 tablespoon water, beating the egg with a fork to create an egg wash.

6. Take the tart crusts out of the oven and egg wash using pastry brush. Reduce heat to 350°F and bake for an additional 30–35 minutes. Set aside on a rack to cool.

7. For the topping, heat the jelly in a small saucepan over low heat until it becomes liquefied. Arrange the raspberries in a crust and drizzle with the warm jelly.

Makes 1 large tart or 4 mini tarts

Truffles

½ CUP LIGHT COCONUT MILK
14 OZ SEMI-SWEET ENJOY LIFE
CHOCOLATE CHIPS
1 ½ TABLESPOONS MARGARINE
3 TABLESPOONS FLAVORING OF
YOUR CHOICE
⅔ CUP THICKENER (FINELY GROUND
NUTS, FLAX SEED, COCONUT
CREAM POWDER, OR RICE BABY
CEREAL)

1. Bring coconut milk to a boil.

2. In a metal bowl combine the chocolate and margarine. Pour the milk over the chocolate and cover for 5 minutes. Using a hand whisk stir the mixture to make sure that all the chocolate has melted.

3. Add flavoring and one of the above mentioned thickeners. Place the mixture in the refrigerator overnight or put in the freezer for an hour.

4. After the mixture is cooled, use a melon scoop to form batter into a ball then roll into a coating of your choice (coconut flakes, cocoa powder, powdered sugar, nuts, etc.).

Makes about 1 dozen

Yellow Cake

2 ½ CUPS FLOUR MIXTURE (SEE P.10)
2 ½ TEASPOONS BAKING POWDER
2 TEASPOONS XANTHAN GUM
½ TEASPOON SALT
⅔ CUP MARGARINE, SOFTENED
1 ¾ CUPS SUGAR
2 EGGS
1 ½ TEASPOONS VANILLA
1 TEASPOON BUTTER EXTRACT
1 ¼ CUPS MILK SUBSTITUTE

1. Preheat oven to 375°F.

2. Grease and flour two 9-inch cake pans or one 13 x 9 inch pan.

3. Combine dry ingredients.

4. Whip margarine with an electric mixer and add sugar. Add vanilla, butter extract, and eggs.

5. Add the dry ingredients alternately with the milk until the batter is smooth. Evenly distribute the batter in pans and bake for 28–30 minutes.

6. Cool and frost with butter cream frosting.

Serves 8–12

Zucchini Bread

3   EGGS, BEATEN
2   CUPS SUGAR
1   CUP VEGETABLE OIL
2   CUPS ZUCCHINI, GRATED COARSELY
     AND WITH PEELS ON
3   CUPS FLOUR MIXTURE (SEE P.10)
1   CUP ALMOND FLOUR (OPTIONAL: IF
     USING, SUBTRACT 1 CUP FLOUR MIX)
1   TEASPOON BAKING SODA
1 ½ TEASPOONS GROUND CINNAMON
1   TEASPOON VANILLA
¼   TEASPOON BAKING POWDER

1. Preheat oven to 350°F.

2. Grease and flour two loaf pans.

3. Blend eggs, sugar, and oil. Add zucchini and vanilla.
    Add cinnamon, baking soda, and baking powder.
    Slowly blend in flours.

4. Pour mixture into loaf pans, evenly divided between
    the two pans. Bake for 50–60 minutes or until
    toothpick comes out clean.

5. Cool on racks for 15 minutes then use a knife to
    scrape the edges of the bread from the pan. Invert on
    wire racks and cool completely.

Makes 2 loafs

Helpful Websites and Books

Asthma and Allergy Foundation of America
http://www.aafa.org

CSN Photography
www.cassinickelson.com

Drug Information
http://www.drugs.com

Entertaining Allergies Website
http://www.entertainingallergies.com

Food Allergy Anaphylaxis Network
http://www.foodallergy.org/about
.html

Food Allergy Initiative
http://www.foodallergyinitiative.org/
section_home.cfm

Food Allergy Survivors Together (FAST)
http://www.angelfire.com/mi/FAST/

Food and Drug Administration, information
on allergies
http://www.cfsan.fda.gov/~dms/wh-alrgy.
html

How to Survive with Multiple Food Allergies
and Eventually Thrive Again
http://www.food-allergy.org/

Medline Plus, information on food allergy
http://www.nlm.nih.gov/medlineplus/
foodallergy.html

Astor, MD, Stephen. *Hidden Food Allergies: Finding The Foods That Cause You Problems and Removing Them From Your Diet.* New York: Avery Publishing Group, 1988.

Fenster, PhD, Carol. *Cooking Free: 200 Flavorful Recipes for People with Food Allergies and Multiple Food Sensitivities.* New York: Penguin Books Ltd., 2005.

Fenster, PhD, Carol. *Special Diet Solutions: Healthy Cooking Without Wheat, Gluten, Dairy, Eggs, Yeast or Refined Sugar.* Littleton, CO: Savory Palate Inc., 1997.

Gioannini, Marilyn. *The Complete Food Allergy Cookbook: The Foods You've Always Loved Without the Ingredients You Can't Have.* New York: Clarkson Potter, 1997.

Kall, Konrad, Bobby Lawrence, and Burton Goldberg. *Allergy Free: An Alternative Medicine Guide.* Boulder, CO: Natural Solutions, 2000.

Haas, Elson and Cameron Stauth. *The False Fat Diet: The Revolutionary 21-Day Program*

for Losing the Weight You Think Is Fat. New York: Ballantine Books, 2001.

Hagman, Bette. *The Gluten-Free Gourmet Bakes Bread: More than 200 Wheat-free Recipes.* New York: Holt Paperbacks, 1999.

Hagman, Bette. *More from the Gluten-Free Gourmet; Delicious Dining without Wheat.* New York: Holt Paperbacks, 2000.

Hills, Hilda Cherry. *Good Food, Milk Free, Grain Free.* New York: McGraw-Hill, 1999.

Reilly, Rebecca and Romulo Yanes. *Gluten-Free Baking: More Than 125 Recipes for Delectable Sweet and Savory Baked Goods, Including Cakes, Pies, Quick Breads, Muffins, Cookies, and Other Delights.* New York: Simon & Schuster, 2007.

White, Suzanne Caciola. *The Daily Bean: 175 Easy and Creative Bean Recipes for Breakfast, Lunch, Dinner and . . . yes, Dessert!* Washington, DC: LifeLine Press, 2004.

Zukin, Jane. *Dairy-Free Cookbook.* New York: Clarkson Potter, 1991.

Recipe Index

Acorn Squash	92
Almond Candies	158
Apple Banana, and Flax Muffins	161
Apple Pear Quinoa Crisp	162
Apple Stuffed Pork Loin	114
Applesauce	95
Aunt Nina's Apple Pastry	31
Baked Chicken	117
Banana Muffins	165
Barbecue Chicken Legs	118
Barbecue Sauce	121
Barbecued Sloppy Joes	122
Basic Crepes	125
Blood Orange Rockfish	126
Bok Choy Soup	60
Bosnian Wedding Soup	63
Bread Sticks	76
Broccoli Salad	96
Caramel Sauce	166
Carrot Cake	169
Carrot Salad	99
Chicken Crepes	129
Chicken Pot Pie	130
Chicken Soup with Dumplings	64
Choco Crinkle Cookies	170
Chocolate Cake	173
Chocolate Chip Cookies	174
Chocolate Covered Carob Brownie	177
Chocolate Mousse	178
Cinnamon Rolls	56
Coconut Crème Brûlée	181
Cranberry Sauce	42
Cream Dried Beef on Toast	133
Cream of Broccoli Soup	67

Cream of Mushroom Soup	68
Creamy Spinach	24
Creamy White Bean Dip	79
Easy Brussels Sprouts	52
Fig Bars	182
Flat Bread	80
Forgotten Cookies	185
Frozen Fruit Drink	186
Fruit Compote Crepes	189
Fudge Brownies	190
Garlic Ginger Soup	71
Giblet Gravy	37
Gingersnap Raspberry Sandwiches	193
Glazed Ham	48
Grand Marnier Cranberry Muffins	194
Greek Bok Choy Topper	83
Guacamole	84
Harvest Soup	41
Herbed Pizza Crust	134
Holiday Stuffing	38
Icing	197
Korn Bread	100
Lamb Patties	137
Leftover Prime Rib Stew	32
Mexican Yellow Rice	103
Mustard Glazed Salmon	138
Orange Rosemary Pound Cake	198
Pancakes	201
Pasta Salad	104
Pavlina's London Bricks	202
Peach Cream Pie	205
Pie Crust	206
Pizza Crust	141
Potato Ravioli	107

Prime Rib	20
Puffed Flat Bread	87
Pumpkin Pie	46
Quirky Coleslaw	108
Raspberry Butter Cookie Sandwich	209
Rhubarb Crisp	210
Rice Pudding	213
Risotto	111
Roasted Potatoes	23
Roasted Turkey	34
Rum Balls	214
Salmon with Minty Mustard	142
Scones	217
Scottish Shortbread	218
Seafood Chowder	72
Seafood Loaf	145
Shepherd's Pie	146
Spiced Apples	55
Steak with Mushrooms	149
Strawberry Ambrosia	221
Stuffed Mushrooms	88
Stuffed Peppers Bosnian Style	150
Sweet Ham Bake	153
Sweet Potato Hash Browns	51
Sweet Potato Pie	28
Sweet Potato Puree	45
Tapioca Pudding	222
Tart Crust	226
Tart Custard	225
Truffles	229
Vegetarian Stuffed Peppers	154
Yellow Cake	230
Yorkshire Pudding	27
Zucchini Bread	233